Metallica
"Talking"

OMNIBUS PRESS

METALLICA *Talking*

Copyright © 1994 Omnibus Press
(A Division of Music Sales Limited)
This edition © 2004 Omnibus Press

Cover & Book designed by Fresh Lemon.
Picture research by Sarah Bacon.

ISBN: 1.84449.099.8
Order No: OP49896

Exclusive Distributors
Book Sales Limited,
8/9 Frith Street, London W1D 3JB, UK.

Music Sales Corporation,
257 Park Avenue South, New York, NY 10010, USA.

Music Sales Pty Limited,
Lisgar House, 30-32 Carrington Street, Sydney, NSW 2000, Australia.

To the Music Trade only:
Music Sales Limited,
8/9, Frith Street, London W1D 3JB, UK.

Photo credits:
All images LFI except:

Front Cover: Mick Hutson / Redferns
Jay Blakesberg / Retna: 96; Danny Clifford / Retna: 133;
Stewart Cook / Rex Features: 110; Ross Halfin / Retna: 113;
Mick Hutson / Redferns: 105, 136; IMA / Rex Features: 70;
Julian Makey / Rex Features: 67; Joseph Marzullo / Retna: 122;
Tony Mottram / Retna: 4; Photoreporters Inc / Rex Features: 119;
Neal Preston / Retna: 29; Frank White: 24, 34, 49, 77, 84 (top),
87, 91, 95, 102, 103 (top), 124; WireImage: 116
Colour Section Picture Credits: Ebet Roberts / Redferns: 1;
Christina Radish / Redferns: 2; Mick Hutson / Redferns: 7

Printed by: Caligraving Limited, Thetford, Norfolk.

A catalogue record for this book is available from the British Library.

Visit Omnibus Press on the web at www.omnibuspress.com

CONTENTS

Metallica Talking. Or should that be Lars Ulrich Talking? Words pour forth from the dynamic Danish drummer's hyperactive cake-hole like the bullets from a Kalashnikov, or the rattling tom-fills during one of the band's more frantic numbers.

Anyone who's ever come within earshot of Metallica off stage will know that it's the diminutive Ulrich who does most of the talking. Lyricist and vocalist James Hetfield only really comes out of his shell on stage, preferring to otherwise lurk in the background in an attempt to preserve some sort of mystique. Lead guitarist Kirk Hammett has even less to say, and is usually content just to let his fingers do the talking. And bassist Jason Newsted, who served with Metallica from 1986-2001, was rarely quoted in the press, still being perceived as the "new boy" even after many years of exemplary service.

Introduction

But Lars... show him a microphone and he'll show you his tonsils – any time, any place, anywhere. You know those drumming bunnies that advertise the batteries with the copper-coloured top on TV? They continue to last up to six times longer than ordinary zinc carbon batteries, right? Well, they've got nothing on our alkaline ally, who'll rabbit-rabbit-rabbit up to sixty times longer than ordinary zinc carbon skin-beaters, the human or floppy eared variety.

Then again, Ulrich has been at the helm of Metallica's extraordinary multi-platinum success ever since he formed the band with Hetfield back in 1981. Both creatively and business-wise Lars is a driving force within the group, the heart of the band [who] beats even faster off stage then he does on it. So perhaps it's only fair that any interview with Metallica should involve at least four C90s full of rabid verbosity delivered in that unique Danish-American drawl of an accent.

As the years have gone by and the beers have gone down, Hetfield, Hammett and Newsted edged more to the fore, so are featured as generously as possible within these pages. Journalists have gone out of their way to secure quotes from Hetfield in particular, not least due to his battle with alcohol abuse that, for a while, seemed to threaten not only his but the band's existence. However, Ulrich sailed back into the fray when Metallica declared war on Internet music 'thieves' Napster, making the file-sharing debate a personal crusade – to, it has to be said, a decidedly mixed fan reaction.

After such weighty matters, replacing Jason Newsted was a piece of cake. Making their mark on the new millennium in 2003 with the chart-scaling *St. Anger* album, Lars, James, Kirk and new boy Robert Trujillo remain as uncompromising, successful and quotable as ever.

INTRODUCTION

In The Beginning

❝Out of all the band, I'm the one who back in 1977 would sit outside Kiss's hotel room in Copenhagen to get their autograph, or wait for Ritchie Blackmore there. Remember, you're talking to the guy who brown-nosed his way through England in 1981 with Lemmy, Diamond Head and Iron Maiden! That side of me has *been* there! That's one of the reasons Metallica exists, because I'd sit there and learn from the Motorheads, Diamond Heads and Iron Maidens, because I was so far up their ass all the time! I've been to Motorhead rehearsals in 1981 – when they were working on the 'Iron Fist' songs – as a punter, absorbing and learning the vibe. That's what made me realise I wanted to do this shit myself!❞ LARS ULRICH, AUGUST 1992

❝It's a little misleading to say we only formed because of the compilation (the *Metal Massacre* album on which Metallica made their debut). If you look at the big picture, then yes. But the short version of a long story is that I'd been looking since about January of '81 to form a band, going through various mutations up to about July '81, when Motorhead came through southern California. I'd got so fed up trying to get a band together that I went to England.❞

LARS ULRICH, FEBRUARY 1991

"We gigged around LA for a year and a half – extremely unsuccessfully! – but the city never really took to us. We were on the same bills as groups like Ratt and Steeler but things just never worked out."

LARS ULRICH, DECEMBER 1984

"I had a great drawing that a friend of mine from Reading, Tony Taylor, had done. He put the word 'Thunderfuck' above it. That was one of the earliest contenders (for a band name). Another one was Helldriver – remember that song from the first Accept album? They were the two main contenders that I had. James had this Leather Charm thing. I think that was the band that he was in before we hooked up, who'd done the original 'Hit The Lights'. I guess we eventually compromised on Metallica."

LARS ULRICH, ON THE EARLY SEARCH FOR AN IDENTITY, FEBRUARY 1993

"We'd done this demo tape ('No Life Till Leather') and I guess copies found their way across to the East Coast. He (mentor Johnny Z) had been promoting gigs out on the East Coast, bands like Venom and stuff. He also had this little stall in a flea market selling records and shit, and he claims that one day these kids were in there playing that Metallica demo, and he dropped everything and grabbed the phone." LARS ULRICH, FEBRUARY 1993

"We were big fans of theirs at the time. It was their first tour and it was pretty cool. It was different from touring in America. All the excesses of touring were much more alive and well in America, and because we were so young we were just out to enjoy ourselves. It was kind of different in the UK, but we still had a lot of fun – a lot of drinking and over-the-top shit was happening all the time. But we were just blown away with how great the gigs were in Europe. We'd never played to thousands of people and it was cool to see how many kids were into our stuff."

**LARS ULRICH, TALKING ABOUT METALLICA'S FIRST
EUROPEAN TOUR WITH VENOM, FEBRUARY 1993**

IN THE BEGINNING „„

❝John Bush (the Armored Saint vocalist once offered the post of singer in Metallica) was just some guy we saw, and for LA he was a 'banging dude. He's a cool singer, great style, but in the end things would've crumbled; he would've left, or whatever.
Then I stopped thinking too much about how it 'should be', and how I 'should be' singing and all that crap. I remember the first time the band kinda realised how my singing should be was on the first demos – 'Jump In The Fire', 'Hit The Lights', 'The Four Horsemen' and 'Motorbreath'. When that song came up I just kinda fucking yelled it, screamed it. Then everyone said, 'Hey man, that's how you should sing the other ones', and I was like, 'Well actually I feel a lot more comfortable singing that way. I never thought you guys would think like that'. And from then on I'd just yell. As far as loosening up and moving around more later on, booze had a helluva lot to do with that. We used to have huge sessions on the 'Kill 'Em All' tour before we went on. I mean, I can't even fucking remember whole tours and shit. That's no good!❞ JAMES HETFIELD, MAY 1990

CLIFF BURTON, KIRK HAMMETT, LARS ULRICH AND JAMES HETFEILD

Dave Mustaine

"It was more or less an attitude problem, not ability. We've tried to patch things up but there's still certain vibes there. It's not something that I want to go into as I still like the guys and I don't want to hurt their success by putting them down or try and make myself look better.

"Basically, when they told me to leave I packed in about 20 seconds and I was gone. I wasn't upset at all as I wanted to start a solo project during the middle of Metallica anyway.

"In the past we had tried to kick both Lars and James out of the band. Lars started to cry because he didn't want to leave and we gave James a second chance because he wasn't too well at the time. But I really care about the guys a lot. They're doing really well and I'm getting money out of this so why should I put them down and hurt my pay roll?"

DAVE MUSTAINE, JUNE 1986

DAVE MUSTAINE

DAVE MUSTAINE

❝I think it's kinda depressing that Kirk (Hammett) got a free ride to number one in your magazine's (*Metal Forces*') readers' poll in '84 because of my guitar solos from the 'No Life Till Leather' demo.❞ DAVE MUSTAINE, JUNE 1986

❝The first thing I wanna clear up is this thing about me playing Dave Mustaine's solos on *Kill 'Em All*. That's total bullshit. What I did was that I was told by the then management to play the first riff in every beat and that's exactly what I did. If you listen to the solos on the album and then listen to the 'No Life Till Leather' demo you'll find that they're completely different. My style is totally different to Dave's. He likes to masturbate on the fretboard, playing 10,000 notes in a small time measure. I don't come from that school of guitar playing, all my notes are thought out. As for him inventing this type of guitar technique, that's bullshit too!**❞** **KIRK HAMMETT, FEBRUARY 1987**

❝The journey out to the East Coast in March '83 to play some shows was simply us throwing all our equipment in a truck and driving to New York. It took a week and there were some incidents with Mustaine on the way that really weren't very pleasant. It kind of showed us that it was a situation which could potentially get silly. It was really the way he was dealing with people around us.
❝So we arrived and met Johnny Z and it was like, 'Hi, nice to meet you, we want to send our guitar player home!' It was a nice shock. We had all these gigs lined up so we couldn't tell him right in advance, we had to tell him he was going to get sent

home. He was so unpredictable that we didn't know if we told him and he hung around for a couple of days whether he'd come after us with a meat cleaver or something. We played a gig and the next morning we'd booked him on a bus home, and had Kirk (Hammett) flying in that afternoon.

"We went in where he was sleeping and woke him up. I was the one who was definitely closest to him at the time and I didn't want to say anything, and as Cliff was the newest member he didn't want to say anything, so we both pointed to James to do the dirty deed. We told him and he looked at us and didn't really know what to do. He was sitting on the bus before I think it hit him. In retrospect, it may have been a dirty way to do it, but he was so unpredictable it was certainly the safest!"

LARS ULRICH, FEBRUARY 1993

"I don't think too many people are into us (Megadeth) because of Metallica, and Metallica's brainwashing the world that I was a headcase and I was a drunk. They kept saying I was washed up. It was hard for me to win those people over again."

DAVE MUSTAINE, AUGUST 1986

"I might as well still be in the band (Metallica) because they're still using my music! 'Leper Messiah' (from *Master Of Puppets*)... I wrote that song! They didn't give me a credit on the record!
"They say I'm a drunk, I can't play guitar. Obviously I can play guitar, and I'm not a drunk or else I'd be slobbering on you right now. I've got my career well in hand. I was thrown out because there was too much personality in the band, too many clashes between James Hetfield and me. If you look at him on stage now, you can see where he got all his charisma from. I can't even be myself on stage because people will be saying I'm ripping off James! But I'd be ripping off myself!" DAVE MUSTAINE, AUGUST 1986

"I was expecting the first (Megadeth) album (*Killing Is My Business... And Business Is Good*) to be a lot like Metallica, but I think it's great that Dave's taken a completely different approach to anything we had done with him." **LARS ULRICH, MAY 1986**

DAVE MUSTAINE

"It wasn't musical problems... I mean, do all the leads, I don't give a shit, I like crunching away in the back. And singing-wise I was happy taking a back seat. So we never stepped on each other musically, it was just personal." JAMES HETFIELD, MAY 1990

"The thing about Dave is that he's so up and down all the time, depending upon the alcohol content in his blood at whatever time he's talking. Sometimes when he's in one of his bad moods he'll say a whole bunch of shit about us, but we're so used to it by now that it doesn't even matter anymore.

"The thing that irritates me though is that in America there's a magazine that is circulating a bunch of 'Metallica versus Megadeth' stories just to sell more magazines. The guy even admitted to me once on the phone that the only reason he was doing it was to sell more magazines. So here I had this guy admitting to me that he actually did it for magazine sales, and meanwhile there's kids in high schools all across America fighting each other because some of them like Metallica and some of them like Megadeth, which to me is complete bullshit, because there's room for all of us.**"** **LARS ULRICH, SEPTEMBER 1988**

"I think that all you have to do is look at the fucking stickers on the albums – 'featuring Dave Mustaine, former member, songwriter and big mouth of Metallica'. I mean, you'd read the word Metallica more in the first three years of that band than you would the word Megadeth. I'm not sitting here trying to take credit for anything. I'm just saying that obviously it has made a difference. But I think that what's cool about it – and I really mean this – is that Dave's been able to take his band from absolute scratch and build it up to a respectable band that's not just another Metallica clone, but is actually doing something unique and original. I mean, the guy is such a fucking character, you just gotta respect him." LARS ULRICH, SEPTEMBER 1988

"Well, I don't really know what to say about Dave...**"**
JAMES HETFIELD, SEPTEMBER 1991

"You want to know the truth? It's comical. Every time I get a magazine that says Megadeth on the cover, that's the first thing I turn to. Let's see what Dave has to say today. Let's see how he can put his size 11s in his mouth again. The funny thing about Dave is every time I see him it's, 'Oh Lars, I said some really bad things about you in some magazine and I'm sorry'. Dave! Fuck it! Relax! He's just on an emotional roller coaster."

LARS ULRICH, SEPTEMBER 1991

"Tell Kirk to call Dave Mustaine. He needs some lessons.**"**

LARS ULRICH, NOVEMBER 1986

"When we first saw their name (Megadeth) on the list of available bands (for Metallica's Milton Keynes shows, June 1992) we started joking about it, until we realised it would be cool to see Dave on the same bill as us. We knew it would either be shit, or lay the whole thing to rest.

"A lot of the shit thrown around was out of his mouth for whatever reasons – drugs or whatever. He's apologised and that's fine, whatever. I mean, I kinda feel sorry for the way he is. I have no problem sitting down and talking with the guy, and I was kinda actually looking forward to it. There were no harsh words, no biting sarcasm. It went fine." JAMES HETFIELD, JULY 1993

Influences

66 We took the power and energy of Motorhead back in '79/'80 and mixed it with more traditional arrangements and riffing, because you can't call Motorhead a riffy band.

66 The other group that inspired us back in '81/'82 was Diamond Head, what they were doing on the *Lightning To The Nations* album. They were a riffy band and the way they arranged their songs influenced James and myself in terms of song writing and structures. 99 **LARS ULRICH, DECEMBER 1984**

66 **Listening to their records now is still an inspiration to me...** 99

LARS ULRICH, TALKING ABOUT
DIAMOND HEAD, NOVEMBER 1987

DIAMOND HEAD

66 I know people regard *Kill 'Em All* as the start of Thrash, but I give full credit to Venom. They started it all. Their first album, *Welcome To Hell*, was so fucking unique when it first hit. And Metallica were obviously heavily influenced by them. 99

LARS ULRICH, SEPTEMBER 1988

66 **One of my favourite bands back then was The Ramones...** 99

LARS ULRICH, DECEMBER 1984

66 I still think of them as one of my all-time favourite British rock bands. 99

LARS ULRICH, REFERRING TO BUDGIE, NOVEMBER 1987

"I don't think I can put into words how much Motorhead meant to me when I first started buying their records and going to their gigs. I remember when they supported Ozzy in the States and me and some friends followed their tour bus around for about six days...**"** LARS ULRICH, NOVEMBER 1987

"I was truly obsessed by the New Wave Of British Heavy Metal.**"**
LARS ULRICH, SEPTEMBER 1988

"I wanted to be Jimi Hendrix... I was one of the handful of people who actually listened to the Sex Pistols. I was always looking for the next extreme.**"**
KIRK HAMMETT, APRIL 1992

"They (Jaguar) greatly influenced Metallica. In fact, the intro to our song 'Whiplash' (on *Kill 'Em All*) was a direct rip-off from their number 'Stormchild', which appears on the *Heavy Metal Heroes* compilation.**"**
LARS ULRICH, SEPTEMBER 1988

"The band was one of my main inspirations in early Metallica."
LARS ULRICH, TALKING ABOUT
DANISH BLACK METAL OUTFIT
MERCYFUL FATE, NOVEMBER 1993

JIMI HENDRIX

INFLUENCES **"**

“One day in junior high somebody bought the first Kiss album. That pretty much changed everything for me. On my 14th birthday I asked for a bass guitar. I wanted to be Gene Simmons.**”**

JASON NEWSTED, APRIL 1992

“I'd get cardboard boxes and paint stirrers and be Ian Paice!” LARS ULRICH, APRIL 1992

“Anyone who's got this record (Samson's 1981 album *Shock Tactics*) will know where we ripped off the sleeve design for our new album, ...*And Justice For All*, from! Er, let me put it this way: I would be lying if I said that I didn't look at this cover when we were thinking of ideas for our own sleeve!**”**

LARS ULRICH, SEPTEMBER 1988

IRON MAIDEN

“They, more than any other band, are responsible for opening up all the doors for Heavy Metal in the '80s... They've never given in, and as a result have been a big inspiration to a band like us, to stick to what we believe in and not just turn out crap to sell records or please radio stations.” LARS ULRICH, PRAISING IRON MAIDEN, NOVEMBER 1987

“Yeah, James has been into this type of music (the work of Italian composer Ennio Morricone, responsible for the soundtracks to films like *A Fistful Of Dollars* and *The Good, The Bad And The Ugly*) for years, and some of the melodies are really impressive. In fact, if you came down to the studio when we record then you'd find Morricone records lying around all over the place. The same with our dressing room on the road. Jason is also into this sort of stuff, so yeah, it has had an influence on us.**”** **LARS ULRICH, FEBRUARY 1992**

The Records

Kill 'Em All

66 'Kill 'Em All' was basically the first ten songs we'd written. What's the point of writing a song that's not good enough to make your record? It (the album) ended up sounding very different to anything that had come out of America. We weren't consciously trying to start anything, we were just doing what came naturally. 99

LARS ULRICH, FEBRUARY 1993

66 We spent six weeks up in Rochester, New York, recording the album at the Music America Studio. The actual studio is in the basement of this huge old colonial-type of club house. It's full of old folk about to drop. Anyway, up on the second floor there's this huge ballroom which is perfect for getting a good drum sound. The only problem is the place is fucking haunted, so I had to have someone else up there the whole time I was recording. My cymbals would start spinning, you know, shit like that. It was scary, but I'd love to record there again.

66 We're really pleased with the way the album has turned out and I think we've given the punters value for money. I mean, side one runs a staggering 25 minutes while the flip clocks in around the same. We used the first nine songs we ever wrote on this album, and we'll use the next nine on the following one, and so on. It's all part of Metallica's plan for World Domination.

66 Anyone who owns the 'No Life Till Leather' demo will be pleased to know that most of the songs on the album are faster, especially 'Motorbreath' and 'Metal Militia'. And we've retitled a track; 'The Mechanix' is now called 'The Four Horsemen', which has even had three and a half minutes added, as have most of the songs. 99 LARS ULRICH, AUGUST 1983

THE RECORDS

❝I really like the cover... The idea of a sledgehammer lying in a pool of blood may sound kinda simple, but it looks real neat...**❞**

LARS ULRICH, AUGUST 1983

❝We didn't know anything about producing or any of that crap, so the whole thing was kind of innocent. A kind of innocence that you can never recapture after your first time in the studio. I remember they wouldn't let us in for any of the mixes or anything like that. I remember hearing the album and going, 'Oh my God, that sucks!'❞

JAMES HETFIELD, NOVEMBER 1992

❝There's a credit on the back of that album that says 'producer'. I think you should erase that and put 'coffee drinker', ha ha ha! I think *Kill 'Em All* shows a very hungry, enthusiastic and honest band. I remember we had some bad experiences at the end. Me and James were staying behind to mix the album with these guys and because they were on such a short budget, when we wanted to come in I think they were afraid that we would want to change it too much and it would take too long. I remember Cliff banging on the fucking studio door and this voice on the intercom saying, 'Oh, you can't come in right now', and you could hear them listening to the mixes on the intercom!**❞** **LARS ULRICH, NOVEMBER 1992**

❝If 'Seek And Destroy' is borrowed from any Diamond Head song, it's 'Dead Reckoning'. It greatly inspired 'Seek And Destroy', shall we say...❞ LARS ULRICH, JUNE 1993

Ride The Lightning

❝I think we're as happy as we could be (with the album). A few of the songs were only written just before we had to do the album, so I think we might have arranged them a little differently if we had had the opportunity to put them down on tape first, and then gone away and listened to them before doing the album.

❝The initial sound problems were really due to all our gear getting ripped off just three weeks before we got to Copenhagen. For instance, James had this one-in-a-million Marshall head that he lost and he had problems getting the rhythm sound that Metallica are known for. We probably went through every Marshall in Denmark, including all of Mercyful Fate's gear, before finding one that was right.**❞** LARS ULRICH, DECEMBER 1984

❝The difference with *Ride The Lightning* compared with *Kill 'Em All* is that it's not just like one complete track like *Kill 'Em All* was, and the way it's different is because not all the tracks are played at 'Metal Militia' speed. You see, the one thing we realised between making *Kill 'Em All* and *Ride The Lightning* was that you don't have to depend on speed to be powerful and heavy; I think songs like 'For Whom The Bell Tolls' and 'Ride The Lightning' reflect that sort of attitude.❞ LARS ULRICH, DECEMBER 1984

❝I believe that, in terms of the songs, the production and the performance, this LP is far superior to anything we've ever recorded. There's a lot more melody in *Ride The Lightning* material; the choruses are more out in the open and the arrangements are much better. We're beginning to broaden our horizons.**❞** LARS ULRICH, JUNE 1984

❝We did that (the album) in Denmark, basically because we were on tour there and we stayed because it was cheap to record. The guy Flemming (Rasmussen) was kind of a producer and engineer, and he did it both for very little money. He introduced us to some stuff and we learnt a lot on that album. Besides the latest album (*Metallica*), *Ride The Lightning* is probably my favourite.❞ JAMES HETFIELD, NOVEMBER 1992

THE RECORDS

"The main difference between *Kill 'Em All* and *Ride The Lightning* was that we had Cliff and Kirk, who brought a whole diversity and new musical edge to the whole thing. We wanted to try to do some different things, not to play 'Whiplash' all the time, which we knew would get boring. We were really proud of the way *Ride The Lightning* came out. We were really thrilled with the sound."

LARS ULRICH, NOVEMBER 1992

"Even though most people say that *Master Of Puppets* was the definitive Metallica album, I think I would probably take *Ride The Lightning* as my most favourite album." LARS ULRICH, MAY 1990

"There was a little hostility in Europe to things like 'Fade To Black', but I think it holds up well today." **LARS ULRICH, FEBRUARY 1993**

"On the *Ride The Lightning* album we learnt that you could still be powerful even if the pace was slowed right down, and now we've understood that you can still hit hard even when there's subtlety in the music." LARS ULRICH, MAY 1986

Master Of Puppets

"With this album it was the first time that we've been recording in the studio where there hasn't been a big red cross on the calendar saying 'The album has to be released on this date!', because of the financial restrictions. So this time I guess we took advantage of the situation and took our time making sure everything was as good as we could get it under the circumstances. I mean, a lot of bands go into the studio, find the right guitar or drum sound and then bash it out, particularly with the first album. But if you listen to *Master Of Puppets* you can hear a lot of different moods and feels, so sometimes we would work for maybe one or two days on just getting the right guitar sound for a specific part of a song.**"** LARS ULRICH, MAY 1986

"I actually feel that we went into the studio a bit before we should've with *Master Of Puppets*..." LARS ULRICH, FEBRUARY 1987

"We're right into using changes of mood and are trying to broaden out our musical base and I think this comes across really well on the new record, where we allow ourselves considerable breathing space and opportunity to go in any direction we chose. This, in some ways, is down to the amount of time and money available for the recording of *Master Of Puppets*. It was the first record where our US label, Elektra, got directly involved and the budget therefore was vastly increased over what went previously.

THE RECORDS

And when there are less restrictions on you in the studio and you're not in a situation of having to rush things because the finances have run out, then you can relax and experiment a bit more. **"**In all honesty, this is the closest we've come yet to something that is genuinely satisfactory. Of course, no artist or musician is completely happy with a product, but in comparative terms *Master Of Puppets* is something we're all proud of.**"** **LARS ULRICH, MAY 1986**

"'Orion' is bits and pieces of other songs thrown together. The bluesy, moody part in the middle was originally the tail end of another song, but we felt it was so strong that it could be the basis of an instrumental as words weren't really needed."

LARS ULRICH, MAY 1986

" 'The Thing That Should Not Be'... that's the heaviest song. It's tuned down to C-sharp, so low that the strings are flapping on the neck!**"**

JASON NEWSTED, JUNE 1993

" It's pretty cool and an alternative to the regular version. It's too bad there wasn't a bit more time to do something about the sleeve. To be honest, myself and the guys didn't know about it until we read it was coming out in *Kerrang!* If we had've known about it earlier we would've definitely made it a little bit different packaging-wise for the fans because it's not much different to the original. " LARS ULRICH, TALKING ABOUT MUSIC FOR NATIONS' RE-RELEASE OF *MASTER OF PUPPETS* AS A DOUBLE ALBUM, FEBRUARY 1987

" We felt inadequate as musicians and as songwriters, and that made us go too far, around the time of *Master Of Puppets* and *...Justice...*, in the direction of trying to prove ourselves. 'We'll do all this weird-ass shit sideways just to prove that we are capable musicians and songwriters'. **"** **LARS ULRICH, NOVEMBER 1991**

" I think, lyrically, that's one of my favourites... The songs took quite a time to get together for that one. We did it in Denmark again. Production wasn't too bad. We mixed it in the States because we ran out of time at the studio. "

JAMES HETFIELD, NOVEMBER 1992

" I remember being really proud of that song '(Welcome Home) Sanitarium'. I remember James singing an actual melody on it and us going, 'Oh my God! We'd better not mix it up so people can hear it!'
" *...Puppets* was the next step in us opening up more. Some of the stuff in 'Orion' is really beautiful. We spent about four months on the album and it brought us up to the next level in America, even though there wasn't the slightest trace of a single on there. It was the album a lot of people took to, what can I say?**"**

LARS ULRICH, NOVEMBER 1992

THE RECORDS

...And Justice For All

❝The fucking thing took two years to make!❞ JAMES HETFIELD, MAY 1990

❝**We're gonna call it *Wild Chicks And Fast Cars And Lots Of Drugs...*❞** LARS ULRICH, MARCH 1988

❝We didn't wanna go through what happened last time, when we booked studio time a few months ahead of ourselves and found that by the time we had to go into the studio some of the songs weren't ready. We were still writing in the studio, which is a waste of time. So this time around we thought we'd be a bit clever and get all the fucking songs ready in advance before booking into the studio. So in mid-October, after the European Monster Of Rock festivals, we began to get the numbers ready, and the most extraordinary thing happened: we penned nine numbers in just eight weeks! That's unheard of in Metallicaland...❞

LARS ULRICH, MARCH 1988

❝**A concept... I don't like that word. A concept to me is something really contrived and premeditated, where you sit down and plan everything out to the smallest detail.**
❝**The justice thing is just something that fits a lot of the album's lyrical content. It's kinda like *Ride The Lightning* and *Master Of Puppets*, where *Ride The Lightning* mostly dealt with death crap and *Master Of Puppets* was more about shit like manipulation and crap like that. This new one has a general theme – definitely staying away from the word 'concept' – running through it which is based on this whole justice thing. We thought it would make a strong album title, so we decided to use it. Plus, what's cool about it is that it's not too direct – people can look at it a lot of different ways, whether it be a bit sarcastic, or a bit humorous, or a bit serious, or what have you.❞**

LARS ULRICH, SEPTEMBER 1988

❝'Blackened': This song is a bit different from all our other opening tracks in that we've purposely avoided the whole over-long, half-hour, huge intro bullshit thing which we've done for a couple of albums now and everyone else seems to be doing it as well. So this song comes out blasting well. So this song comes out blasting at you from the word go.

" Musically, it's also a bit different from what one would consider to be a typical Metallica opening track, because it takes a couple of sharp turns later on in the song and becomes almost like a full-circle type of thing. It just sort of goes from one extreme to another and then back again.

" Lyrically, this one's about the good old Mother Earth and how she's not doing too well nowadays. It's just about all the shit that's going on in the world right now, and how the whole environment that we're living in is slowly deteriorating into a shithole. This is not meant to be a huge environment statement or anything like that, it's just a harsh look at what's going on around us.

" '...And Justice For All': This one is something like ten minutes long. It also goes through some different shit along the way, with various feels and a lot of changes. It's pretty uppety-tempo for the most part, but it's a little different for us in that the main riff is centred around this weird drum beat that I came up with in the rehearsal studio one day. It's not even a straightforward kind of beat, it's more like a sideways-type of thing with a lot of tom-action and stuff, but it sounded cool so we used it.

" It's about the court systems in the US where it seems like no one is even concerned with finding out the truth any more. It's becoming more and more like one lawyer versus another-type situation, where the best lawyer can alter justice in any way he wants.

" 'Harvester Of Sorrow': Compared to some of the other songs on the new album it's a bit more basic

THE RECORDS 99

and more instant, I would say. It's a real heavy, bouncy, groovy type of thing. Plus, it's not too long by Metallica standards - it's only about five and a half minutes long!

"Lyrically, this song is about someone who leads a normal 9-5 type of life, has a wife and three kids, and all of a sudden, one day, he just snaps and starts killing the people around him. It's not a pretty subject, I guess...

"'The Shortest Straw': This one is a very energetic, uptempo sort of thing. It's not the fastest song on the album, but it's definitely a lot more aggressive than some of the other things on the record.

"It deals with the whole blacklisting thing that took place in the '50s, where anyone whose view was a little out of the ordinary was immediately labelled as a potential threat to society. There were all these people in Hollywood whose views didn't fit in with the mainstream, and they were all shoved out of the entertainment industry because of their beliefs.

"'To Live Is To Die': This is our obligatory instrumental on the new album. Compared to our previous instrumentals, 'The Call Of Ktuku' and 'Orion', this one's a lot huger and more majestic sounding. It's also a lot looser in some ways in that it's a bit more of a jam-type of thing and not quite as square as some of the instrumental stuff we'd done in the past.

"A lot of people might give us flak about this one because it features some riffs written by Cliff (Burton) a few months before he was killed – just like they gave us flak for using Dave Mustaine's stuff – but the truth of the matter is, these riffs were just so huge and so Metallica-sounding that we had to use them. We're certainly not trying to dwell on Cliff's death or anything like that, we're simply using the best ideas we had available, and this was one of them.

"'Eye Of The Beholder': This one is a bit more mid-tempo, a bit simpler than some of the other stuff on the album. It's got some real heavy, mid-tempo riffing and it's a real groovy type of thing.

"The lyrics to this one are pretty much self-explanatory. It's basically about people interfering with your way of thought and how America is really maybe not as free as people think.

"'Frayed Ends Of Sanity': It's a bit more musical and intricate than most of the other songs on the album. It's got a pretty long musical middle part with a lot of changes and some pretty cool melodies.

Overall it's pretty much a mid-paced sort of thing, but it's really intricate and it might take a couple of listens before you can get into it.

" Lyrically, it's really just about paranoia – you know, being afraid, but not really knowing what you're afraid of.

" 'One': That's one about someone who has no limbs, no speech, no sight, no hearing and is basically just a living brain. It's about what sort of thoughts you would have if you were placed in that kind of situation. It's actually a lyrical idea that we had a couple of years ago, but we never got around to using it before.

" Musically, it's a bit mellower than some of the other shit. It's a bit more of a build-up sort of thing. It starts out for a couple of minutes with some really mellow, clean, acoustic guitars with ballad-type singing over it before building into this huge middle section which is more of an epic sort of thing, and then it just sort of speeds up and ends like a runaway freight train.

" 'Dyer's Eve': It's basically about this kid who's been hidden from the real world by his parents the whole time while he was growing up, and now that he's in the real world he can't cope with it and is contemplating suicide. It's basically a letter from this kid to his parents asking them why they didn't expose him to the real world and why they kept him hidden for so long. It's a real heavy subject and our management is sure that trouble is on the way. But we like it, so...**"** LARS ULRICH, SEPTEMBER 1988

THE RECORDS 99

"I had about 72 different running orders written on a Federal Express envelope at my house... I lost three days' sleep because I knew that people would rip it apart. Then I went back and realised that this stuff was written that way, and I also realised that I was fucking with the basic thing that Metallica is all about – following gut instincts." LARS ULRICH, AUGUST 1988

"The general reaction has been very encouraging. But it's definitely one of those albums you need to spend a lot of time with; it's not the sort of thing you can put on in the background and then go and cook breakfast or have a wank. You have to listen to it because there's so much shit going on in the songs. If you don't pay attention it won't sound anything more than a bunch of riffs.

"I personally feel that albums where the initial reaction is something of a question tend to be the ones that last a lot longer. But it doesn't surprise me that people's first reaction is to go, 'WHAAAT?' Maybe that's a good thing.

"But basically I'm so confident with it I feel almost bullet-proof at the moment. This is the first time there have been no compromises, either song-wise or time-wise."

LARS ULRICH, AUGUST 1988

"One thing that I think we went for this time around when we were mixing the album is a very up-front, in-your -face type sound. We approached it in a way that was very similar to what we did on the $5.98 EP, in the sense that we wanted all the instruments to practically jump out of the speakers and slap you in the face while you're listening to it.

"Obviously the album is gonna end up sounding a lot better than the EP because we spent more time on it and it's a lot more serious than the EP. But they both have that dry, in-your-face type feeling to them, which we like.

"When I listen to *Master Of Puppets* now, it sounds like it's coming from about a mile behind the speakers – it sounds really distant. But this new album, everything just hits you in the face all at once." LARS ULRICH, SEPTEMBER 1988

"It's different. We consciously tried to make it a lot deeper than *Master Of Puppets*, especially after the *Garage Days* thing. We wanted harder sounds and we realised we could get more impact by not using reverb and echo, that kind of thing. What we've created here leaps out in a way that *Master Of Puppets* did not; I listen to that album now and it's like a wet noodle."

LARS ULRICH, AUGUST 1988

"Me and Jason were listening to 'Dyer's Eve' down at the rehearsal studio about three weeks ago and, well, it's pretty fucking progressive! I don't think in our wildest imagination it would be possible for us to write a more progressive song than 'Dyer's Eve'.

"Listening to the album now it's obviously very much a rhythm guitar and drum-sounding album, and I think that what we've been getting into in the last few months and listening to the Queen song we did, that most of the people who were asking where the low end was on the ...*Justice*... album will not be as disappointed on the next album.

"I must admit that listening to ...*Justice*... now, I do wonder why we put three minute intros onto some of the stuff. Obviously that's what we were into at the time, but right now I'm more into the song writing style we had on *Ride The Lightning*.

"I also know a lot of people found ...*Justice*... difficult to get into, but I'm not gonna sit here and apologise for that. I mean, out of all the Metallica albums to date it's no secret that ...*Justice*... is by far the less accessible of them all. I just find it funny that it's sold better than the others by three to one."

LARS ULRICH, MAY 1990

THE RECORDS

METALLICA *Talking*

“A lot of the riffs (on the album) came out slow and heavy because we were into slower, heavier shit at that time. We got tired of playing fast, uptempo stuff.” JAMES HETFIELD, MAY 1990

“When they (the record company) started whinging on about a single it was the obvious choice, because it wasn't 14 minutes long and didn't have 39 silly time changes.”
LARS ULRICH, REFERRING TO 'HARVESTER OF SORROW', AUGUST 1988

“With ... *Justice* ... I think we went for something we didn't really achieve. We wanted a really up-front, in-your-face album and it didn't really work out. The drums are fucking awful, there's no depth to it. I mean, people come up with all these concepts on why it sounded like it did, like 'Oh, you can turn the volume way up and it doesn't distort'. Ha ha! I don't know what the fuck we were doing, but back then we liked it for some reason.”
JAMES HETFIELD, AUGUST 1991

“This time the attention wasn't focused so much on the musicianship, with everyone running off in different directions. It was more to do with the songs and vibe.” LARS ULRICH, AUGUST 1988

“We probably could have made another 12 good songs out of all those riffs on ... *Justice* ..., just spread them out a little more.”
JAMES HETFIELD, NOVEMBER 1991

"It's a very bleak album. I can see now that it's the one album where we took it too far. The songs were too progressive and long. But the point is that when we made the record it was what we wanted to do. You should never second guess. I feel it's the album that has aged least well, but I'm still amazed at some of the playing on it. Bands like UK or ELP would have been proud of the progressive nature of some of the playing!"

LARS ULRICH, FEBRUARY 1993

"I think the songs are good, but I think we got a little too fancy with shit. I think there's some good riffs on there, but they're spoiled by the length of the songs. I think the lyrics are really good. I think the production sucks." **JAMES HETFIELD, NOVEMBER 1992**

"For the last couple of weeks I've been sitting and talking about *...And Justice For All* for 15 minutes. I don't want to turn every interview into a negative criticism of ... *Justice* ..., because at the end of the day that record had a lot of good aspects too. And I'm sure that record can stand the test of time. When we did the album it felt right, but it surprises me how soon after I walked out of the studio I started questioning it."

LARS ULRICH, SEPTEMBER 1991

"The other day in Italy there were these two guys just drilling into this whole thing about 'One' and anti-war, and making a statement of peace for the kids. 'You guys care so much'. I was telling James about this afterwards. We were laughing. 'Why do people make such a big deal about it?' And James turns round and goes, 'All it is, is a fucking song about a guy who steps on a land mine!' That kinda sums the whole thing up." **LARS ULRICH, NOVEMBER 1991**

"Touring behind it (the ... *Justice* ... album), we realised that the general consensus was that the songs were too fucking long. Everyone would have these long faces, and I'd think, 'Goddamn, they're not enjoying it as much as we are. If it wasn't for the big bang at the end of the song...' I can remember getting offstage one night after playing ... *Justice* ... and one of us saying, 'Fuck, that's the last time we ever play that fucking song!'" KIRK HAMMETT, NOVEMBER 1991

THE RECORDS

Metallica

❝I've heard Bon Jovi this, Bon Jovi that, but the fact of the matter is, (producer) Bob Rock's got an incredible ear for attitude and feeling. Now that we've worked with him on pre-production, he's got us kicking ourselves for not doing certain things sooner.

❝Bob's convinced that the four of us playing together has a certain magic or vibe that never happens with me doing drums to a click track and James coming in and overdubbing rhythm guitars, blah blah blah. We've been very proud of how musically accurate our records have been in the past and how in tune everything's been, but it's gotten so clean and antiseptic that you've got to wear gloves to put the damn thing in the CD player!

❝This time around it'll probably have more of a feel of what we're after when we're playing live; a lot looser, groovier, underplayed and overplayed when I want it to be. Being incredibly precise and accurate worked for a while. I'd like to try something different for a change.

❝I think one of our major mistakes in the past has been sitting fucking with the stuff, concentrating on too many details, being too particular... This time it's got a generally looser, livelier attitude, which I hope will be a welcome contrast to the last album being so mechanical.

❝All I can say is that we're letting the riffs speak for themselves for a change rather than diluting them with all the progressive nuances of ... *Justice* .... It sticks to one thing rather than fucking around needlessly.❞

LARS ULRICH, OCTOBER 1990

THE RECORDS

" Many people have asked me, 'What will your fans think of this record?' And I think most of our real fans know that we want to play many different styles of music and that's something that we started doing on the *Ride The Lightning* album. We just have to keep doing things to make it interesting. I don't want a band like... no, I wanted to say Judas Priest, but I think the thing with Iron Maiden was a little misunderstood. I'm one of Maiden's biggest fans. I have said good things about Maiden in interviews for the past eight years. They're one of my favourite bands, but it's more or less the same, and people expect that. That's why a lot of people like Iron Maiden. But I don't want to be in a situation where you have to give people what they expect from you. " LARS ULRICH, SEPTEMBER 1991

" I was thinking the other day about this album not being as dark as the last one. I mean, you basically can't get any darker than ... *Justice* .... *Justice* ... was the epitome of the darkest, deepest basement album. It's a little too early to say if this record is optimistic... " **LARS ULRICH, FEBRUARY 1991**

" What we started doing this time, more than ever before, is really working a lot more with the vocals. I'm not necessarily talking about lyrics and shit, I'm talking about vocal melodies. The vocal thing, in the past, always remained a mystery to everyone in the band but James, because he'd write everything five minutes before he'd sing it in the studio. We're treating the vocals on this record with the same up-front attention as the guitars, bass and drums. We've got all these demo tapes lying around with James going, 'Na na na, na na na na'... " LARS ULRICH, JANUARY 1991

" It's very strange because I think finally we're going for a less mechanical and more attitude thing this time around. We're going for this attitude and this vibe in the playing that we've never had before. It's like we're finally starting to realise that we've all hit a stride in our music, and it's really cool. " **LARS ULRICH, MAY 1991**

" We knew we couldn't write another ... *Justice* ..., so we went for a simpler approach. But these songs may only have a couple of riffs throughout, which means you have to make the song more

interesting with the other elements. For instance, the vocals have to do a lot more carrying on this album, the same with the solos and the little guitar harmony things. So just because the basic songs are simpler, doesn't mean we've put any less into them.**

JAMES HETFIELD, AUGUST 1991

We definitely put 110 percent into this one, and that's what we got out.

JAMES HETFIELD, NOVEMBER 1992

I can recall the first time I heard that song ('Nothing Else Matters'). We'd done these UK shows in May of last year (1990) and afterwards we were going to have a break for a couple of weeks before we'd meet up again and continue writing. James gave me a tape of some shit he'd been working on and I'd gone back to Copenhagen and was listening to this tape when the core of 'Nothing Else Matters' came on and I just lost it. It was so huge, and when I met up with James I said 'we've gotta go to work on this one right away.' A lot of people are going to be surprised when they hear this song, but to me it just sounded so right and a natural thing to do. LARS ULRICH, AUGUST 1991

Bob (Rock, producer) has got this theory that, in the past, Metallica has always written a bunch of songs and then just gone in and recorded them and left. He wants to try and, y'know, when we're done with the solos and the vocals and stuff like that, spend a couple of weeks on just production shit. We don't really know a lot about that. Just more like trying to layer some of the songs with guitar shit and kinda doing some texturing and other crap like that, which is new territory for us. **LARS ULRICH, AUGUST 1991**

THE RECORDS

"We were listening to the track ('Nothing Else Matters') in the studio and (producer) Bob Rock suggested we added some strings in there. So he got in touch with Michael Kamen, who used to do all the string arrangements for bands like Pink Floyd back in the Seventies, and he does various film scores too. It's funny because when Bob Rock mentioned this guy Michael Kamen he never meant Jack Shit to me, then a couple of days later I was watching this movie on video, *Lethal Weapon*, and in the credits it had '...all music conducted and arranged by Michael Kamen!' All of a sudden this guy's name kept cropping up everywhere, so we thought, 'Fuck it, let's just go for it'.

"Anyway, we sent him a copy of the song and it came back about a week later and we put it on expecting, y'know, a couple of violin bits here and there, and... well, he recorded a fucking 30-piece symphony orchestra down at Abbey Road Studios in London! There were violins, cellos, violas, double basses, woodwind instruments... 30 fucking guys playing 'Nothing Else Matters'! We were fucking floored! Actually, we felt he'd gone a step too far, because we wanted to retain the original vibe of the song, so in the end we found a good balance, and although the orchestra is still in there, it doesn't take over the song. I'm really proud of it." LARS ULRICH, AUGUST 1991

"This time nothing came up, idea-wise, that was good enough to write a song like 'Whiplash' or 'Dyer's Eve'. Although if you listen to the album there are a couple of songs that have fast guitar riffs – like, say 'Through The Never', that maybe eight years ago I would have done all the gallopy drum shit and the song would've turned out fast, but now I hear things differently and... well, I guess if people now think we're playing too slow then they should send all the hate mail to me!" **LARS ULRICH, AUGUST 1991**

"The overall vibe on this record, going all the way back to the song writing and everything, was to just simplify things. Back some time ago there was this onslaught of Heavy Metal albums that came out, and everybody was putting out titles and covers with clever wordplay and all these paradoxes and phrases where,

y'know, everything was change a couple of letters
around or come up with all these cool titles and all
this stuff. Heavy Metal of late has this real cartoon
kinda vibe to it. We're basically gonna go as far in the
opposite direction of that as we can... This time around
I think we just really feel that it's like, 'Here's 12 songs,
here's like an hour's worth of new Metallica music, and here
are some great lyrics from James, and that's it', y'know. **"**

LARS ULRICH, AUGUST 1991

" Bob (Rock, producer) should be given total credit for making James
feel comfortable enough to take that guard down and really sing
(on the album). We've always thought of ourselves as Big Bad
Metallica, but Bob taught us a new word none of us had ever heard
before – soulful. As for James' image as a singer now, well, Chris
Isaak is his new hero. **"** **LARS ULRICH, OCTOBER 1991**

" Some of the material on the new record came from riff tapes
recorded five years ago. As long as we keep churning out stuff
then maybe some of the material that wasn't ready in July '91 will
be on the record we make in 1996! What happened this time after
we picked the riffs was, Lars has a room in his house where he
and James put the stuff together and get a rough arrangement.
Then I'd go in. Then Kirk. Then, with Bob Rock, we'd go to
rehearsal. Then we went into One On One (LA studios) and
started recording. We were all there for each other during the
recording, and it shows. We were very focused and had our shit
together. **"** JASON NEWSTED, NOVEMBER 1991

" On this album I thought out my solos a lot more than I have in the
past. I'd listen to the song, and instead of sitting down with the
guitar I'd sing out ideas into my tape recorder. I thought a lot about
what direction I wanted to take with the solos. **"**

KIRK HAMMETT, NOVEMBER 1991

" This album is a little easier to listen to for people who'd never
heard Metallica before. **"** JAMES HETFIELD, NOVEMBER 1991

THE RECORDS **"**

"I've been listening to a lot of the blues since the
...*Justice*... album three years ago, and it's definitely
reflected in my playing this time around. This record has more
of a 3-D approach instead of a one-dimensional bass thing."

JASON NEWSTED, NOVEMBER 1991

"I've run into fans who think the album's crap. Friends of mine
who are really hardcore fans have said, 'Well the album's not as
heavy. You guys aren't as heavy as you used to be'. I go, 'Man,
you're trying to tell me 'Sad But True' isn't heavy? 'Holier Than
Thou' isn't heavy? How do you define heavy?'"

KIRK HAMMETT, NOVEMBER 1991

"This record is very unified, and we worked really hard at getting
that point across." JAMES HETFIELD, NOVEMBER 1991

"It just feels right. We've set ourselves up to be ridiculed, but if
we were afraid of being ridiculed we would have played the game
a lot differently. We threw a Metallica logo on it and it pretty
much titled itself. It's a case of, 'Here's the record, here's the lyric
sheet, you figure it out'. You can call the album anything you
want: *The Black Album*, *The Snake Album*, *Metallica Sucks*...
Actually that's one of my favourite titles. One of the guys from
Guns n' Roses told me they were toying with the idea of calling
their next record *Guns n' Roses Suck*, and I said, 'If you're not
gonna use it...!'" LARS ULRICH, NOVEMBER 1991

"'The Unforgiven' is one (of my favourite tracks on the album).
It's about a guy who never really takes advantage of certain
situations, never really takes any chances. Then, later on in life, he
regrets not having done anything with his life, so he dubs the rest
of the world 'the unforgiven'. There's a simple aspect to a lot of
these songs, and those were pretty hard on us to write. We can
write the 100-riffs-in-one-minute songs, but our challenge this time
was to write a simple song and make it mean and thick as shit."

JAMES HETFIELD, NOVEMBER 1991

"('The God That Failed' is) a personal song for James. It's about this mind-washing Christian Science stuff, where people think they can go around medicine and be healed of their ills. I know some people will say, 'The God That Failed'... isn't that about Satan?' No, it's not that at all." LARS ULRICH, APRIL 1991

"This is about people who take their responsibility on their shoulders but find out the people they think they represent aren't really behind them at all. Does that make sense? We wrote it around Jason's bass line, sort of like Aerosmith's 'Sweet Emotion'.**" LARS ULRICH, TALKING ABOUT 'MY FRIEND OF MISERY', APRIL 1991**

"I always find that the first song you write for an album has a certain magic to it, and that was 'Enter Sandman'. This song just has such a feel to it that we felt it should be the first new thing people heard. It's one of the easiest songs we've ever written. If you're gonna narrow it down, it's about nightmares from a little kid's point of view...

THE RECORDS

66 I have a personal hard-on for 'Enter Sandman'. 'Sad But True' has a really cool feel to it. 'Holier Than Thou' and 'The Unforgiven' are both really cool. 'Nothing Else Matters' is something kinda different for us, and that's one of my favourites too. 99

LARS ULRICH, NOVEMBER 1991

66 I think that song ('Sad But True') is gonna be in our set for a long, long time. The mood it creates is different from any other song on the record. 'Sad But True' has the heaviest silence of any song we've ever recorded. Hear the silence. It's loud, isn't it? 99 **JASON NEWSTED, FEBRUARY 1992**

66 At the middle of the song ('Sad But True'), where it stops for six counts, you're just waiting for it to come back. It's cool and it's different for us. There's a lot of that shit happening on this record. We learned how not to fill every space with music or guitar or whatever. You're not going full-out all the time. It's just growing up, man, and learning how to write and play cool shit. A lot of people just stop and knock their head against the wall and do the same album three or four times in a row. That's shit. 99 JAMES HETFIELD, FEBRUARY 1992

66 People have been saying to me, 'Why are there no speed songs on the album?' And I really didn't actually think about that until people started telling me. I just realised that every time I heard a fast guitar riff I wanted it to 'swing' a little more. So every time there was a fast guitar riff I put a 'half-time' on it. I think it still has the energy, but it also has a little more shit into it. So you can blame it on me. 99 **LARS ULRICH, SEPTEMBER 1991**

"We took a lot of chances on this record. Like the slower songs, where James is singing and it's all pretty guitars and real clear picking and stuff... people weren't expecting that. It's cool, because it shows another side to Metallica."

JASON NEWSTED, FEBRUARY 1992

"'Nothing Else Matters' is definitely one of the highlights for me... When the basic idea for 'Nothing Else Matters' came on (Hetfield's demo tape) it was the first thing that really knocked me out. I think James has been a little underestimated as a singer. People will always talk about him as a frontman, and, you know, fuck, shit, cunt, piss and all this kinda stuff. But finally I think he won't be underestimated as a singer anymore.**"** **LARS ULRICH, SEPTEMBER 1991**

"We wanted a song that wasn't your typical Metallica ballad. 'Fade To Black', '(Welcome Home) Sanitarium'... they all start mellow, then the chorus is big, then the verse is mellow... We wanted to build it a little more vocally, bring in other guitars. I think the string arrangement on it is pretty fucking cool. If we're going to go for this kind of song we might as well go all the way."

JAMES HETFIELD, TALKING ABOUT 'NOTHING ELSE MATTERS', SEPTEMBER 1991

"Because of the fact that there was a new producer, because of the fact that we said in some interviews that the songs were shorter, blah, blah, blah... people took these little bits of information and sort of conjured up these images and got into a frenzy. We had to keep it in perspective that these were the next songs, and that we were just trying to make the album the best that we could. If you start thinking about how everyone hypes it to be the next super-mega-event and all that, you could lose your mind.**"**

LARS ULRICH, APRIL 1992

"It ('Enter Sandman') is quite the simplest song we've ever written. If you look at the song closely there's really only one riff in it. The whole song is built around one riff. Which is, I think, an incredible thing to say about a Metallica song!"

LARS ULRICH, SEPTEMBER 1991

THE RECORDS

❝I think we pushed all that progressive stuff. We could do two things: we could repeat ourselves or we could do something else. When things become very obvious, we kinda step away from it. And it just became really obvious to us that we'd had enough of this progressive stuff, all this 'ten riffs in each song' stuff. And it's a lot of fun playing simple songs, it really is.❞

LARS ULRICH, SEPTEMBER 1991

❝**Our main concern is always good songs, and we've just written a lot of good songs this time. Also, hooking up with the right producer, to get them on tape good. I mean, it's a lot easier to listen to. It has a fuller sound, it's got a lot more muscle to it.**

❝**As for Bob Rock as producer, well, you know, there's always people who will shoot something down before it's even started, and they're the close-minded ones. They just look at the track record of what he's done before, which is unfair. Though if you do go back and look at the stuff he's produced, it sounds great, even though the songs were crap and the bands were fucking gay!❞**

JAMES HETFIELD, NOVEMBER 1992

❝The lyrics are a bit more personal this time around. On *...Justice...* the whole process was disjointed, especially towards the end. We were mixing while out on tour. The material was what we were into at the time, but looking back... We could never do two albums in a row that fall into the progressive direction. This album is a lot bigger sounding.❞ **KIRK HAMMETT, NOVEMBER 1991**

❝When I brought in the lyrics (to 'Holier Than Thou') Bob Rock said, 'Hey, is this song about me?' He got real paranoid. It's more or less about the typical rock ligging that goes on. Slipping in through the door because of name-dropping and shit like that.❞

JAMES HETFIELD, SEPTEMBER 1991

❝'My Friend Of Misery' is one of my favourites. 'Sad But True' is also one of my favourites, because of its Black Sabbath feel. 'Don't Tread On Me' is also one of the songs that I really like. But there isn't one I don't like. It's 12 very strong songs with their own unique feel and mood. They each create their own identity.

❝James surprised us all with his singing this time around. Whether it's his out-and-out ability to double his guitar parts or double his vocal parts or come up with amazing lyrics, he never ceases to amaze us.❞ **JASON NEWSTED, NOVEMBER 1991**

❝Getting the things from within was a lot harder and more gratifying in the end for me. On the ... *Justice* **... album it was more of a socially conscious-type thing. I found it was too easy to sit down and watch CNN and go, 'Oh, oil spill - there's a song!' Trying to dig stuff out was more of a challenge, and we're always up for challenges.❞** LARS ULRICH, APRIL 1992

❝It is kind of amazing to think that we have, you know, the best selling album of the Nineties so far. It's just constantly selling, that's the thing. That's kind of how we've built our career, to have longevity, you know? This one's reaching out to a few more folks this time, instead of selling in one large chunk...❞

JAMES HETFIELD, NOVEMBER 1992

❝You know, it's not really untitled, you can call it whatever you want. Like *Led Zeppelin IV*, **or whatever.❞**

LARS ULRICH, SEPTEMBER 1991

❝I got to tell you that what I'm most proud of, for myself, is that it's now almost 16 months since the release of the album and it still sounds and feels as good as it did when we finished it.

THE RECORDS

On ... *Justice* ... there were things that started freaking me out very quickly, but every time I hear this one it blows me away how good it sounds. I mean, there's nothing on the album that's really started to annoy me yet. **" LARS ULRICH, NOVEMBER 1992**

Garage Days EP

" Heavy Metal companies in Europe prefer to have 'unavailable anywhere else' type shit on the B-sides of singles. Now we're not a band who likes to submit our own songs solely for B-sides because we like to have them on albums. So we just went into the studio and knocked out a couple of cover songs (Diamond Head's 'Am I Evil' and Blitzkrieg's 'Blitzkrieg'). They're the only two cover songs that we still play at rehearsals or live for the seventh encore! **"**

LARS ULRICH, DECEMBER 1984

" We've taken a whole bunch of strange shit recorded by some other bands and breathed death into them! We went into the studio four days ago, laid down the tracks, and now we've got a couple of days to mix the thing. I mean, we didn't fuck around here! Straight in, bang, bang, bang, and out again! No shit!

" Also, what I think is great, is that this will be our first release under our new European deal with Phonogram Records. And just in case people are dumb enough to think that landing a deal with a major label means we're about to change our ways and play things safe, we've decided to do the most off-the-wall thing we could, which is this EP!

" We've thought about doing something like this for a long time, but we've never really had the opportunity before. And wait till you hear how we've done some of these things! I mean, we went out of our way to make sure we had a weird bunch of shit to work on... We've taken some strange things that these other bands did and given them the full Metallica treatment! This is still a fucking Metallica record, we just weren't responsible for writing the songs... "

LARS ULRICH, COMMENTING ON THE *GARAGE DAYS...* EP, JULY 1987

❝It's very important that people know that this is a fun thing and has nothing to do with albums or anything.**❞**

LARS ULRICH, AGAIN TALKING ABOUT
GARAGE DAYS..., AUGUST 1987

❝Well, it wasn't as blatant as some bands do it (releasing the 'One' single as a 7", 12", CD, limited edition poster version, etc.) I mean, it's not as though there were 13 different coloured vinyl versions or something. At least we tried to do it tastefully and give everyone a different track with each format, and I think the special roadie version which has a demo version of 'One' and an eight-page insert which has 'A Day In The Life Of Our Friendly Backline Crew'... that is something that hasn't been done before. So, I think the way it was done was OK.❞

LARS ULRICH, MAY 1989

❝*Garage Days...* was our first dealing with Phonogram over here (the UK). We thought... well, actually it was their idea, to kick it off by doing some cover songs, and we said, 'Well, why don't we just do a whole EP of the shit?' No one's really done that before. Plus, we wanted to keep things low key because maybe people would have said, 'Oh, they're on Phonogram now, big rock band, forget it', and all this bullshit.**❞ JAMES HETFIELD, NOVEMBER 1992**

❝This may sound really contrived, but one of the fun things about being in Metallica is doing something and then a couple of years later somebody else does it. At the time, nobody had done anything like that and now every band and their brother is releasing four, five song EPs full of covers. *Garage Days...* was just a fun thing to do.❞ LARS ULRICH, NOVEMBER 1992

THE RECORDS

66As you know it's very difficult in England, where the music industry works in weird ways in having to have 12 different formats of singles and shit. And as much as we like to go, 'Well, we're Metallica and we don't like to fuck the fans around and stuff', sometimes you have to play by the rules of every different country. See, the record company will argue that there are people who are into collecting different versions and shaped discs and shit, so why shouldn't we make it available to the people who are interested in getting this stuff? Anyway, the idea of this box set crap came up and, well, we decided to go along with it.

66I don't know if many people know this, but when record companies release all these different coloured vinyl and shaped discs, more often than not the band doesn't get any royalties on sales because they are so expensive to manufacture, so really they're just looked upon as promotional items. I mean, the bottom line is, if you already have the regular EPs and just want the new live tracks, then don't buy it, tape it off your friends!99

LARS ULRICH, TALKING ABOUT *THE GOOD, THE BAD AND THE LIVE:*
***THE SIX-AND-A-HALF YEAR ANNIVERSARY 12" COLLECTION*, MAY 1990**

66It's Metallica doing a clean sweep of the attic. We've got all this stuff lying around. We thought, instead of just doing a live album, what can we do that's a pretty cool package? If you want it, you get six or seven hours of Metallica! It's going to be about as big a chunk of any band you've ever been able to buy – like *The Godfather* trilogy, or something!99 LARS ULRICH, JUNE 1993

"It's a boxed set with videos and tapes or CDs. Instead of putting out 17 different versions of tapes, CDs and videos, we'll have one box and that's it. We'll have a whole show from San Diego in January 1992 and half an hour from ...*And Justice For All*, when we had the statue and did things we don't play any more. We'll have three and a half hours of video. We'll have a whole show from Mexico City in March of this year with different songs and performances. So there will be a full show from early in the tour and one from later in the tour, and more photos than you can shake a stick at. It's something for the fans who've been with us for years. It's not the kind of thing people who just discovered us will be into.**"**

LARS ULRICH, OCTOBER 1993

"Looking around and seeing what other bands have done - a single video, a single CD and a double CD, a third CD with two different posters and bonus live tracks – I feel that's ripping people off. What we're doing is saying, 'Here it is, take it or leave it'. And the reason it costs so much (£75) is not so us and Phonogram can walk away with big fat bank accounts, it's basically to cover the fucking costs.

"Our management did a survey and discovered that this is the most expensive packaging anybody has ever put together. You've got everything in there: nine hours of music, a 72-page booklet, backstage passes, stencil, keys to our houses... so fuck it, take it or leave it!" LARS ULRICH, NOVEMBER 1993

THE RECORDS **"**

Load & Re-Load

"In the five years between the Black Album (*Metallica*) and *Load* we've grown a lot individually. So now, coming back together, we've got to put up with a little more shit from each other, and we've got to have a little respect."
JAMES HETFIELD, OCTOBER 1996

"*Load* was the working title of one of the songs... we were looking for a word that had a lot of meanings, that could mean 20 different things, that fits in with the vagueness of the whole record. That's more thought-provoking..."
LARS ULRICH, APRIL 1996

"We started writing about six months ago and that turned into a waterfall, an endless cornucopia of ideas that kept on coming out. It's going very quickly but the key word is relaxed. We're going in and basically doing what we hoped for in our wildest imaginations, which is not getting caught in some anal torment of precision and tightness. The new songs called for a looser, livelier type of thing, and we set our goal to capture the spirit of the songs."
LARS ULRICH, AUGUST 1995

"For the first time we're doing what 98 per cent of other bands do – putting the bass down right on the drums and then the guitar after that. Kirk is playing rhythm guitar for the first time, also. That adds a lot of character to it. The last album was great, but this one is a bit more real." JASON NEWSTED, MARCH 1996

THE RECORDS

“Sharing the guitar parts with Kirk brings him more into the picture, gives him a little more responsibility. He's got his own part going. Live, he's not copying the riff I'm playing, he's got his responsibility to uphold now. It's very healthy, I think.” **JAMES HETFIELD, APRIL 1996**

“On the last album we wrote the best songs first and when we got to song ten we started to fizzle out. This album the pattern was different – song ten was just as good as the first one we wrote. We kind of kept going, ended up writing 32 songs and recording 29 of them. For the first time we went into the studio not knowing what we were going to do. We feel we have at least 25 killer songs.” KIRK HAMMETT, APRIL 1996

“The song '2x4' took on the feel of, uh, smashing someone with a piece of wood, y'know? Instead of trying to out-think someone, just out-smash 'em. Hatred is a big part of my life, and has been for a long while. It's easier to find something to hate than something to like.” **JAMES HETFIELD, MAY 1996**

“When we started the last record with (producer) Bob Rock, we'd known each other six weeks. When we started this record we knew each other five years. We understand each other a lot better. We're a lot more tolerant of each other and I think overall there has been a fraction of the problems that there were on the first record.”

LARS ULRICH, APRIL 1996

“We put out an album (*Metallica*) and suddenly we were surrounded by the mainstream. With this album we're back out at the edges. James put it very succinctly.

He said, 'We're being hated again and I kinda like it.' I can totally relate to that.**" KIRK HAMMETT, OCTOBER 1996**

"I certainly didn't expect *Load* to be as successful as Metallica. Timing has something to do with everything that goes on. If you look at what was happening in '91 with us and Guns n' Roses, before Nirvana, before Pearl Jam, it was the right thing at the right time. If the Black Album (*Metallica*) came out tomorrow I don't think it'd do 60 million copies."

LARS ULRICH, JANUARY 1997

"If Cliff was still in the band, we'd have recorded *Load* a lot sooner. He was very melodically inclined and listened to a lot of melodic music – and this was back in 1984, when the rest of the band were listening to heavy metal 24 hours a day!**" KIRK HAMMETT, AUGUST 1997**

"There was a German group that did some of our songs and the first time I heard it I was shocked. But there was a certain unnamed member of this group who, when he heard what they had done, made the CD player travel into the wall. "We ended up giving this track ('Until It Sleeps') to Moby... but this time we threw it at the wall and kept it."

LARS ULRICH ON DANCE REMIXES OF METALLICA SONGS, MAY 1996

"That's a thing I wanted to try and it didn't work. I can't listen to 'em. I don't know anything about that shit. I can tolerate them, but it still sucks. It was an experiment. I was thinking it was going to be industrial with a real angry feel to it, but it wasn't as heavy as I thought...**" JAMES HETFIELD, OCTOBER 1996**

"This is not album seven, it's the second part of album six. When you've got that amount of material you can do a double album or do what U2 did. Spread it out into two separate records. The material is evenly strong and I hope we're gonna put it all out. "It's more (one-dimensional than *Load*), it'll be 10 or 12 five-minute songs that are all fairly heavy. No 10-minute epics, or James going off on his country tangent."

LARS ULRICH ON 'RE-LOAD', JANUARY 1997

THE RECORDS

"Getting *Re-Load* done was pretty surprising to me – the fact that we stuck to our guns, not adding a bunch of new shit, and got those songs out there. I'm feeling pretty good about that."

JAMES HETFIELD, DECEMBER 1997

"We've started to listen to a lot of very different types of music. I got heavily into blues and jazz. Bringing in all these influences definitely changes all our ways of thinking, and that's basically why *Re-Load* sounds so different... we're different people now." KIRK HAMMETT, AUGUST 1997

"It's the first time a woman's sung on a Metallica album... except for Kirk." **JAMES HETFIELD ON MARIANNE FAITHFULL'S GUEST VOCAL ON 'THE MEMORY REMAINS'**

"The vocabulary of guitar licks that are on our previous albums are used up. I can't recycle them, so I have to come up with something different. I've finally had to sit in a corner, take a deep breath and just play to find a different approach. But I'm happy at how well it's clicked." KIRK HAMMETT, NOVEMBER 1997

"If you record a double album it only counts as one on your contract, whereas this way it counts as two... we get to the pot of gold at the end even quicker!" **LARS ULRICH, AUGUST 1997**

"There's stuff on this album that's as classic as Led Zeppelin and Black Sabbath. That's the thing with Metallica. It's not just another project for me. It's the chance to work with a band I consider to be the new Led Zeppelin or the Beatles. They're pretty much the Bob Dylan of this generation. Let's face facts – it's not Mötley Crüe who are gonna go down in the history books...**"**

PRODUCER BOB ROCK, NOVEMBER 1997

"The lyrics are a lot darker, if we can get any darker! There's songs about being down and out and not accepting pity. Nothing goes your way all the time and that's just life, my friend. People don't take responsibility for themselves and that's always been a major theme of mine.**"** **JAMES HETFIELD, NOVEMBER 1997**

Garage Inc

"There's a side of Metallica that's basically OPM – other people's material. It's one we've enjoyed since the day we started. There's 15 or 20 of those songs floating around now, and we thought we'd put them all out in a set instead of making kids pay $15 for a shitty bootleg.

THE RECORDS

"We just didn't know what we were doing. We'd have some basic ideas, like what Blue Oyster Cult song can we play? We'll talk about it for three hours. We had some things we knew we were going to go in and fuck with, but until we got there, well... We operate spur-of-the-moment creatively. We gave ourselves three weeks to get it done, then the record company had a month to get it out." **LARS ULRICH ON COVERS, OCTOBER 1998**

"There was a vibe between all of us – let's just fucking go for it. The drums were done fairly quickly. The guitars may not be perfect, for sure, but it doesn't matter. (Nick Cave's) 'Loverman' came out as natural as it could have done, one take late at night and a couple of the punk ones were the same."

JAMES HETFIELD, DECEMBER 1998

"I heard Bob Seger's 'Turn The Page' on US classic rock radio and thought that James might sing it really well. No disrespect to Bob, I'm sure he's a nice guy, but he means nothing to me – this is a case of the song over the artist. The lyrics, the bleakness and the vibe had Metallica all over them; it could have been on one of the *Load* albums."

LARS ULRICH, DECEMBER 1998

"The Mercyful Fate stuff was fun, but Black Sabbath are my favourite band ever and Geezer Butler is my favourite bassist of all time, so needless to say doing 'Sabbra Cadabra' was the shit. That was the one I tried my hardest to be ultra-respectful on – my one chance to give a shot out to Geezer."

JASON NEWSTED, DECEMBER 1998

66 'Whiskey In The Jar' was one of the toughest songs to do – we tried to do it four or five different ways, as a ballad or as a real metal thing. The only way we could get it to work was like Social Distortion, which James is really into. A lot of people in America are really psyched up about it, and it's gonna be the next single there. 99

LARS ULRICH, DECEMBER 1998

S&M Orchestral Project

66 We've always tried to write big, epic stuff throughout our career, so this collaboration will be the ultimate conclusion. It would be very nice to have a new song for the shows, so Lars and I may write one in the next couple of months. 99

**JAMES HETFIELD ON METALLICA'S
COLLABORATION WITH THE SAN FRANCISCO
SYMPHONY ORCHESTRA, JANUARY 1999**

66 **It's really in keeping with the spirit of Metallica. For many years we have tried to push ourselves as a band in different directions and this represents another challenge and a logical step for us.** 99

LARS ULRICH, JANUARY 1999

CONDUCTOR MICHAEL KAMEN

66 I say let Metallica be Metallica and let the Symphony be the Symphony. The two have more in common than not. Metallica's music has often had elements of composers like Wagner and Brahms. But they'll need to go full-tilt to be heard over a 100-piece orchestra! 99 **CONDUCTOR MICHAEL KAMEN, JANUARY 1999**

THE RECORDS

"These things get put in front of us and we just jump at them. You either worry about it or make it up as we go along. We seem to be getting better at the latter. I think we always operate better when we operate instinctively. It's like a dare. People have asked what are we going to do, what are we going to wear? You know, I have no idea..." LARS ULRICH, APRIL 1999

"We came up with a couple of new things. Maybe the first one has the Symphony in mind, but the other one is pure Metallica. They're both very fresh sounding, but they're very different from each other as well.**"**

JAMES HETFIELD ON THE FIRST NEW SONGS SINCE *LOAD*, APRIL 1999

"A week ago we didn't have two new songs, a week later we do. We're not the kind of guys with acoustic guitars laying around on the couch who pick up a guitar at 3 am and churn one out. So it's weird, having not written any songs for four or five years, to have to sit there and clutch at straws and turn something out."

LARS ULRICH, APRIL 1999

"It's such a special thing. Usually we go out and tour for 18 months, five million people see us, and here's the live album. But we'll be playing to 6,500 people over two days and a lot of people who are quite interested won't be there. Unless we fall on our ass, there'll be an album – we have the film crew and the recording crew there – but it's not something we'll take on the road and tour for years.**"**

LARS ULRICH, APRIL 1999

"Did you hear the one about the rock band who wanted to play a gig with the Symphony? Well, you're looking at it!"

JAMES HETFIELD'S STAGE INTRODUCTION, MAY 1999

"I find when you do something like that, the reality of the moment becomes really thick and all-encompassing. Other than sex, it's as focused as mind or body ever becomes. Even though I was on-stage with the three other guys, Michael Kamen, the 4,000 people in the hall, the orchestra, the tape machines, the cameras...

they weren't there. During the performance, I realised the need to hold down my end of it, not let anyone down.

"I didn't hear any tapes for almost three months because I wanted to come back fresh without any recollection of what I felt when I was playing it. By reviewing the tapes we've got a better sense of what worked. It's one more layer of things that this band can do, and I think that's been the best thing about this experience – having it as one of the things we can pull out of our sleeve.**"**

LARS ULRICH, OCTOBER 1999

"On the actual nights I was absolutely amazed at how great it felt. It was totally awe-inspiring, and turned our music into symphonic pieces. Everything sounded so much bigger... and so much heavier! We still have to listen to the tapes of our mobile truck recordings and the film footage, but there's a pretty good possibility that we might release it. As to whether it'll be a single or a double or whatever it's too early to say. We did 18 or 19 songs a night, the regular Metallica live set. We might leave some songs off or do the entire concert." KIRK HAMMETT, JUNE 1999

"The new songs we played were literally only about two or three weeks old. 'Minus Human' is a pretty heavy one, it definitely has its moments. 'No Leaf Clover' is more melodic and pretty catchy – it has a great hookline to it. It feels like these songs came out of nowhere because they were so new when we played them. The next album could take a left turn at any point when we get together...**"**

KIRK HAMMETT, JULY 1999

THE RECORDS

"We're staying in London. Whether it's a drive in a van or a helicopter ride to the venue depends on the traffic situation. I guess it would be quite a vibe to stay in the Milton Keynes Travel Lodge, but before a show it probably wouldn't provide the most relaxing of times."

JAMES HETFIELD ON THE MILTON KEYNES "BIG DAY OUT" SHOW, JULY 1999

"If we don't do stuff like 'Sad But True' and 'Enter Sandman' we'd be tarred and feathered – that's cool, you have to keep the pool heated. But playing 'For Whom The Bell Tolls' 60 nights in a row doesn't erect the penis any more. That's why we did the US club tour last year, playing songs no one had ever heard."

LARS ULRICH ON THE SAME SHOW, MARCH 1999

"I've got to rub a little local dirt on my boots for good luck. That started a few years ago at festivals – we'd walk to the stage and I'd get my boots all dirty. Then we started doing indoor shows, and I'd make our wardrobe girl go out and dig some dirt into a box. Hur, hur! Gives her something to do..."

JAMES HETFIELD ON PLAYING LIVE, JULY 1999

"We always like to have bands with us who we can laugh at or laugh with. I'm not a big fan of Marilyn Manson's music but those guys are always fun. I respect Manson. He's smart and it's important that there are guys like him around. Would I let him baby-sit my son, Myles? Sure... rather him than most people I know!"

LARS ULRICH, MARCH 1999

"It's one big day of therapy. It's definitely one of your more aggressive shows. Whatever festival we're doing we add a little bit of angst to it. There's a little more release from us and the crowd. There'll be a few explosions here and there – you gotta have firecrackers to keep everyone awake!"

JAMES HETFIELD ON THE MILTON KEYNES "BIG DAY OUT SHOW", JULY 1999

"I've been very, very open with people about this project. It's not about credibility, or helping unsigned friends of mine – it's about finding bands that will sell shitloads of records. Some people may find that crass, but that's okay – I can't lie about it. I thought I might have to make compromises to find bands that can sell a lot of records, but what I'm finding (is) the bands that I'm looking to sign are also bands I dig. So it's not just a commercial venture, it's one of passion also..." **LARS ULRICH ON HIS RECORD LABEL, AUGUST 1998**

"We have two bands: DDT sound like a more accessible version of Faith No More with two lead singers, and Gaudie are from Texas and sound like a poppier Radiohead." LARS ULRICH, DECEMBER 1998

"James and I play rhythm guitar on a cover of David Bowie's 'Fame'. We're two of many musicians on that album: there's Rob Zombie, Jim Martin, Fred Durst, Tom Morell and more. We've been friends with Primus for a long time – we're always hanging out together and in each other's beds!"

KIRK HAMMETT ON GUESTING ON PRIMUS'S *ANTI-POP* ALBUM, JUNE 1999

THE RECORDS

St. Anger

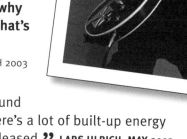

❝There's a lot of bullshit that comes in the wake of what we do. But when all that goes away and it's the four of us in the room playing music that's when everything dissipates. And the experience we had making this record was just awesome. It was amazing.❞

LARS ULRICH, MAY 2003

❝**We'd be jamming songs, and someone would say, 'Don't sing that part, why don't you yell it?' So that's what I did.**❞

JAMES HETFIELD, MARCH 2003

❝We've been sitting around for three years and there's a lot of built-up energy which needed to be released.❞ **LARS ULRICH, MAY 2003**

❝**We've gone through so much experimentation that the more manic stuff crept in subtly. I'd like people to be expecting our take on something like Sigur Ros because when they hit the wall after hearing the first track they'll be pleasantly surprised.**❞

LARS ULRICH, FEBRUARY 2003

❝To now have a record that we're very excited about and a tour that everyone is raving about is amazing.❞ **LARS ULRICH, MAY 2003**

❝**I thing anger had bad rap. It has these connotations that something bad is gonna happen or something is gonna break, but for me anger is a good healthy way without degrading or injuring another person. It's definitely an energy we all feed off.**❞

JAMES HETFIELD, JUNE 2003

"This album (*St. Anger*) is so chock full of energy, and lyrically, it is deeper than it's ever been because it is involving all the other guys.**"** JAMES HETFIELD, MARCH 2003

"The reason there are no solos on the album is because it just felt like that would have taken away from the collaborative nature of the songs. It's not about solos, it's about the four of us moving together musically. And if one more person asks me about that then I'm going to fucking scream!" KIRK HAMMETT, MAY 2003

"For a long time I resisted things like the speed, because I thought it was something we'd already done, and I didn't want to go backwards. But I don't think we have gone backwards. The one thing I would say about this album (*St. Anger*) is that it isn't a return to anything. I want to be quite clear about that. This is new for us. And I hope new for people who listen to it.**"**

LARS ULRICH, MARCH 2003

"*St. Anger* is fast, heavy, aggressive and raw."

LARS ULRICH, MARCH 2003

"I sent a copy (of *St. Anger*) to a friend of mine in Denmark and he rang me back saying, 'This isn't the band that did the symphony record!' Well hey, no fucking shit, this is heavy metal!**"**

LARS ULRICH, JUNE 2003

"To me 'St. Anger' references some of those past moments but it's in a completely new environment. It brings me back to those classic days mainly because it's so fast."

KIRK HAMMETT, JUNE 2003

THE RECORDS

"As a kid, intimidation was a great defence for me to not have to get close to people or communicate or express my fears and weaknesses. So going into Metallica as the staunch statue of a frontman, that intimidation factor blossomed and was a great defensive weapon. I could keep people at bay with that, and not state what I actually needed. That's what *St. Anger* really means to me; being able to express anger in a healthy way, instead of just shutting up and being intimidating and then raging out on someone when it all builds up." JAMES HETFIELD, AUGUST 2003

"Coffee table rock? That's a horrible term! I think *St. Anger* is very definitely an anti-coffee table rock. It's anti-nu metal, anti-pop, anti-everything record. People tell me it has punk elements but that freaks me a bit. Punk these days seems to be about a marketing tool, a look, an image, whereas to me punk is very old school, very anti-establishment 'Do It Yourself' attitude. But, to me, this is metal in '03 - we've raised the stakes that bit where everyone else has to follow." KIRK HAMMETT, JUNE 2003

"Having completed the journey I'd like to think that *St. Anger* is a total celebration of the fact that we can get our heads down and make some incredible music. What you hear is an unbridled flow of creativity." **KIRK HAMMETT, JUNE 2003**

"You know that game curling, with the guys on the ice sweeping with brushes in front of that thing? Well, curling's a good metaphor for what we've been doing. We tried to not obstruct where the music would take us, protecting it from any outside infiltration, so it's a new thing on every fucking front possible."
LARS ULRICH, FEBRUARY 2003

"Because of the way the songs were put together, we would jam, then everything would go into Pro Tools (music production computer software), and we would just move stuff around until we had a song. Then we would work on the song, and once it was done we'd have a nice little ditty on our hands. But we never actually played the songs together as a band."
JAMES HETFIELD, AUGUST 2003

"

"We don't need to go around hugging each other to prove to ourselves what good friends we are."

"Anyone who says they don't want to see their record in the chart is full of shit!"

"Metallica isn't ready to turn into some nostalgic shit."

"We're trying to educate people to the fact that what they're doing is wrong."

"On *Kill 'Em All* we were very angry young men, and now we're very angry middle aged-men." KIRK HAMMETT, AUGUST 2003

"What happened in our childhoods is part of our mental foundation, and tapping into it in a positive way is something we've found out how to do in the last two years. And that is the sound of *St. Anger.***"**
KIRK HAMMETT, AUGUST 2003

"I think we've always done what we wanted to do at any given time. In retrospect, the *Load/Re-Load* stuff could have used a little bit of editing. Up to *St. Anger*, every single song Metallica has written has been on an album, so when James and I ended up writing 29 songs for that album in the fall of '95 we were damn well going to put all 29 on the album. Now in retrospect I ask could the world have done with 12 or 15 less of those? Probably, but back then we didn't have an edit button on our instrument panel. I'm aware that say 'Prince Charming' and 'Attitude' might not be up to some of the other stuff, but if that's as bad as it's going to get when our legacy is written, I'm okay with that." LARS ULRICH, JUNE 2003

"I remember someone giving me a St Christopher way back in the *Ride The Lightening* days and it took me years more to discover that he was the patron saint for the protection of travellers. When I came out of rehab it really hit home that we didn't have a patron saint of anger. And if there wasn't one, dammit, Metallica were gonna create one!**"** JAMES HETFIELD, JUNE 2003

THE RECORDS

"I haven't been this proud of an album since *The Black Album*. The *Load* and *Re-Load* era for us was such a reaction to our first five albums. We didn't want to do what we had been doing: play fast, over the top and aggressive. If anything, the *Load* and *Re-Load* era was a big experiment in hard rock. We needed to do these two albums for us to make *St. Anger*. If we had made *St. Anger* in the mid-nineties, it wouldn't have been as fresh and exciting for us as it is now. It would have felt like doing the same old thing.
"We needed to balance it out. When we finally got around playing fast and aggressive again, it sounded fresh. You need to get to point A to be able to make point B sound better."

KIRK HAMMETT, JUNE 2003

"Once we were over the initial hump of taking the piss out of ourselves we were like, 'hey, that sounds real good' and then it started feeling real in a fresh new way.**" JAMES HETFIELD, JUNE 2003**

"We picked which songs we wanted to take to the next level, but there's other stuff that we put on the back burner, – some ballads, some experimental stuff which is almost like Nine Inch Nails with drum loops – which sounded good. In five year's time it'll be interesting to see what we do with that, whether on another album or on some archival shit we put together."

LARS ULRICH, JUNE 2003

"Lars played Fred Durst four songs off our new album and the next week Fred postponed the release of the new Limp Bizkit album and started rewriting it. Lars and I were talking about it: 'Did he postpone it because he wasn't satisfied with it, or did he postpone it because he heard our direction and wanted to be contemporary with it?' It's interesting. We'll see.**" KIRK HAMMETT, JUNE 2003**

Lyrics

66 Most bands in this area of rock do tend to spit out banal words about Satan, death and rock'n'roll, and I'll admit that on *Kill 'Em All* we were equally as guilty. The lyrics were all written in the plural/'we' form and dealt with subjects such as 'rock'n'roll all night', 'kick ass' and 'let's party'. But we've developed a lot and most of the numbers here (on 'Ride The Lightning') have very personal messages in the singular/'I' form.

66 For example, the title track deals with the electric chair and the fear it can generate, while 'Fade To Black' is about someone who gives up on life, and 'Trapped Under Ice' is to do with cryogenics, y'know, the science of freezing someone's body into suspended animation and then defrosting/waking them up many years later. We have consciously moved away from the traditional clichés of Heavy Metal because if you stick with old images you're doomed to obscurity. 99 **LARS ULRICH, JUNE 1984**

66 **There's a meaning behind Metallica's lyrics. Yeah, there's some darkness. But James is writing about things that can affect him. 'Disposable Heroes', for instance, is about a kid who grew up in a military atmosphere and the army sent him to war and he only comes back when there's nothing more he can do for them, so the army says about this 21-year-old kid to his family, 'Here you can have him back, he's a veg, he's no use to us any more'.** 99

JASON NEWSTED, FEBRUARY 1987

66 I mean, people are saying, 'How come you always write about death?' and shit like that. And then, 'Oh, now Cliff's died you're not gonna sing about death and stuff, huh?' It was anything that consciously came up, we're just curious about shit. 99

JAMES HETFIELD, MAY 1990

"The lyrics... yeah, they're pretty personal."

JAMES HETFIELD, MARCH 1991

"Things are so deep and people are always trying to read shit into things that are real simple. Some people try and tell you what the songs are about and it bores me to death.**"**

JAMES HETFIELD, MAY 1990

"We went through our CNN years, as we call it, where me and James would sit on the couch and watch CNN and go. 'Yeah, we can write a song about this new political turmoil'. The political thing has been played out. Some of the things on the last album (...And Justice For All) were things that pissed me off. I'd read about the blacklisting thing, we'd get a title, 'The Shortest Straw', and a song would come out of that. "This time (Metallica) the songs are the result of what's been lingering in James. You can look around for things that make you mad and you write about them. This time it's a matter of looking within, the experiences you've been through."**

LARS ULRICH, NOVEMBER 1991

"Like a lot of what James writes, even if you have the lyrics in front of you, there's still so many possibilities in there. That's the greatest thing about his lyrics.**" LARS ULRICH, NOVEMBER 1991**

"Whether it's '...Sanitarium' or 'One', the lyrics have something in them that each kid can relate to in their own little piece of the world. We've always maintained an eye-to-eye relationship with our fans, and even though we've sold a lot of records and gotten more popular, the fans have always stuck behind us."

JASON NEWSTED, NOVEMBER 1991

LYRICS

“We are regarded in the US by the likes of *Rolling Stone* and *Time* magazines as the Thinking Man's Heavy Metal band. We are seen by them as a serious band, and all they want to do is talk about the profound implications of our lyrics!” LARS ULRICH, FEBRUARY 1992

“'Don't Tread On Me' (from *Metallica*) is about the flag, basically. Not the United States flag, but the snake flag, one of the first revolutionary flags we had. It's basically a historical song.

“We never hopped onto any bandwagon when the war (in the Persian Gulf) started. People see the word 'war' in a song and they freak. We were getting calls to do that 'Give Peace A Chance' video. Peace off, motherfucker! If you ask me, I don't think this band was really against this war. When I told people that, they freaked. Especially the ones who wanted us to do that video. It's like the new trend was all hippy, dippy, peace, love, this and that. But then, when we started crushing the Iraqis, people got all patriotic all of a sudden. And I thought, 'Yeah OK, as long as it's a blowout, cool. As long as our guys don't die, fuck it!'

“Back to the song though, it says 'war', but the line is: 'To secure peace is to prepare for war', which is a quote from the 1880s, or something. It's basically about how the snake became the logo.”

JAMES HETFIELD, FEBRUARY 1992

"I like the animalistic part of man and nature. I don't know, sometimes I look around and see all the crap that we've accumulated. I mean, what the fuck do we need all this shit for anyway? This song ('Of Wolf And Man') essentially brings things back to the basics, back to the meaning of life. The song illustrates the similarities between wolves and men, and there are similarities.**"**

JAMES HETFIELD, FEBRUARY 1992

"One person started complaining about his personal life, and then another person said, 'Well, I'm having problems too'. And then a third person said, 'Well, goddamn it, I am too!' It wasn't something that was influenced by each other at all. And when we were having these problems with our personal lives it made us realise how much of a foundation the band is for us."

KIRK HAMMETT, TALKING ABOUT THE INSPIRATION BEHIND THE LYRICS
TO 'WHEREVER I MAY ROAM', APRIL 1992

"People always categorise us as this new conscientious band or whatever, but fuck that shit! I hate whiners and I certainly don't want to be labelled as one of them. It doesn't bother me that people say 'They're aware of what's going on', that's fine. But when they start taking a stance for us as far as going, 'Oh, they think that way and that's what kind of band they are', it doesn't mean fuck. I don't wanna be labelled as hippies of the '90s, political activists... I don't like that shit. Who's to say what intelligent lyrics are? We're just writing about what we think's going on, what we wanna write about, what's bugging us, or whatever...

"This band's always been selfish. We're a selfish band, we just write what we wanna and people can take it as they want. It's not like we're selfish in the way of sitting around and talking about ourselves, or hearing people talk about us, we're selfish in the way that we do shit for ourselves and it's always been like that. We're into the self-gratification.**"** JAMES HETFIELD, MAY 1990

LYRICS

The Bass Men

"I'm not sure Ron (McGovney, original bassist) was the kind of guy to make the commitment and take the kind of chances that you do to make it a full-time thing in the band. He had his little job, his little house and stuff and I'm not sure he was ready to go for it and I think we could all sense that.

"So when we saw this guy Cliff with a band called Trauma at a San Francisco Bay Area night then it really became apparent we should try and get him in the band." **LARS ULRICH, FEBRUARY 1993**

"I got over the shock of Cliff's death some time back. Obviously we regret him not being with us, but we're sure his spirit is never far from the band. Being on stage with Jason felt really good from the start and he's fitting in well. I just wish that he'd relax a bit more at photo sessions. Every time he poses he looks like someone from Anthrax!" LARS ULRICH, NOVEMBER 1986

"It (Cliff's death) never really got to me too bad until about two or three nights into that tour. We were sitting in the bar at the hotel and got really wrecked. We'd never really done anything Keith Moon-ish, but we went and tore this bathroom to pieces and kind of got it out of our system that night. From then on it kind of got the physical side of the pain out of our system."

LARS ULRICH, FEBRUARY 1993

"His (Jason's) playing is a little different to his predecessor's – and I'm not knocking Cliff here – in that the guitar and the bass are more a unit now, rather than being separate entities. We encouraged him not to play too much in places, to lay back, kind of get a groove thing." LARS ULRICH, AUGUST 1988

"The main difference between Jason's and Cliff's writing is that Jason tends to write a lot more with the guitar in mind, whereas Cliff's stuff was always like really weird and off-the-wall. If anything, I think that Jason's stuff is a lot closer to James' and my song writing than Cliff's shit ever was." **LARS ULRICH, SEPTEMBER 1988**

"Jason is kinda the stable guy in the middle who holds everything together..." LARS ULRICH, AUGUST 1991

"When we did get together he (Cliff Burton) definitely taught me a lot of stuff. A lot of the classical training he had rubbed off on me, there's no doubt. I got into it and dug it." **JAMES HETFIELD, MAY 1990**

"We've told everybody that Jason is gay, and the first thing anyone says to him is: 'Is it true?'"

JAMES HETFIELD, NOVEMBER 1986

"In order to ease Jason into the band we charged everything to his room. He just treated everyone to a nice night out."

LARS ULRICH, NOVEMBER 1986

"When we arrived in Tokyo all these kids gave us gifts. Jason didn't get any though, they thought he was part of the road crew. So he had a temper tantrum. Poor guy, maybe we should have got him a T-shirt with the statement: 'I'm Jason, Dammit. Gimme A Gift!'" LARS ULRICH, NOVEMBER 1986

THE BASS MEN

"Cliff had input on about a third of the songs, and there was huge pressure on Jason back then to write. But I think he's gotten over it and we've all helped each other through it. As far as the material shit goes, Jason didn't push his way through with his songs, but now he's got a lot more input than on the ... *Justice* ... shit.

"At the start we looked at Jason kinda different because we just wanted to get right back into things without grieving and all that shit. We had some dates coming up that we wanted to get through, so he helped us through that shit. It wasn't like, 'You're in the band now, oh, heeey buddy, how are ya?' There was a lot of leeriness – 'Who is this guy? What's he about?' – getting to know him. But he was so eager and shit, and that gave us all a kick.

"Those auditions for Cliff's replacement were weird, fans were coming up and auditioning... Jason was a fan, but he was a good musician with his own shit going on and everything. Some fans would just audition so they could say, 'I auditioned for Metallica', and that shit got old real quick. There were people outside with recorders going, 'Here I am, I've just auditioned with Metallica'. Needless to say a few tape recorders and faces got smashed, ha ha ha! Those people were just taking advantage. If they were real fans why would they wanna waste our time?" JAMES HETFIELD, MAY 1990

"Jason is great at being sensible; he's the one to know when something's gone too far. I bounce a lot of ideas off him."
LARS ULRICH, AUGUST 1992

"I guess the bass guitar has always been this weird instrument in the band, it's always been overlooked, because with Cliff (Burton)... he was always off on Planet 9. I mean, there were always times when me and James would try and get Cliff to adapt his bass playing a little differently, but Cliff was Cliff and he just done it in his own way and that was that. With Jason I guess we misfired on ... *Justice* ..., but this time around I didn't want to make the same mistake again, so very early on we steered the bass more towards the drum kit and shied away from the guitar a little." LARS ULRICH, AUGUST 1991

"There's actually gonna be some nice bass on this album (*Metallica*). Y'know, bass and Metallica – they're not usually things that have gone well together. But for Album Five it looks like they're finally gonna work it out. I think a lot of it had to do with the fact that, in the song writing, the bass was always identical to what James was doing on the guitar. It took us eight years to figure out that the bass doesn't have to play identical to what the guitar does, especially with drums kinda taking more of a backseat on this album. Jason's playing a lot more with me and we're establishing a sort of, dare I use the term, rhythm section."

LARS ULRICH, AUGUST 1991

"The first few years it was hard for them (the band) to open up and let me into their lives. Cliff was such a big influence on all of their lives. As for his musical abilities, he showed James harmonies, melodies, things about theory that James never knew. He was like a big brother/teacher. I didn't even know him, but now I hang out with some of his friends who are now my friends.

"As a person he didn't really say a lot, but when the serious shit was going down and he did say something, everyone else would just shut up. His words had weight. For him to be taken away

THE BASS MEN

from them, and for some new guy to try to fill his shoes over on the right hand side of the stage, was really tough. It was hard for them to open up to another guy. I tried to deal with it and just be quiet when I should be, do my thing and just try to be me, without worrying how Cliff did things.

"Little by little it's worked out. Over the past year and a half it's become really cool. I really feel like a huge part of Metallica now. We've become real friends." **JASON NEWSTED, NOVEMBER 1991**

"Cliff was responsible for a lot of the things that happened between *Kill 'Em All* and *Ride The Lightning*. I think the biggest maturity or change or growth was between *Kill 'Em All* and *Ride The Lightning*, and most of that was down to the fact that all the songs on *Kill 'Em All* were written before Cliff and Kirk were in the band. So when Cliff and Kirk joined, especially Cliff, Cliff really exposed me and James to a whole new musical horizon of harmonies and melodies, just a whole new kind of thing, and obviously that's something that greatly influenced our song writing abilities on *Master Of Puppets* and *...And Justice For All*. It's something that's still with us, so from that point of view I'd obviously say 'yes' (to the notion that Cliff's influence on the band is still strong).

"On the ... *Justice* ... album there were still some bits left over from some of Cliff's old tapes and stuff, so I mean, Cliff was with us really up through ... *Justice* .... On this album (*Metallica*) there aren't any specific, direct things that I can think of, but the whole way that me and James write songs together, I mean, that was shaped when Cliff was in the band, and was very much shaped around Cliff's musical input; the way he really taught us about harmonies and melodies and that kind of stuff. I mean I don't want to sound corny, but his vibe is always with us, and he was certainly a big part of the whole way that we got our chops together in the early days, about our attitudes and our musical vibe and our everything. He was a great part of the way Metallica has turned out, even after he is no longer with us."

LARS ULRICH, FEBRUARY 1992

Videos

"Look, I suppose for a lot of bands this sort of thing would be seen as something of a tribute, but that's not the way we see it. Basically, it's a 90-minute look-back at the period when Cliff was with us, more of a video documentary taking in Metallica Mks I and II. It's the video equivalent to the recent $5.98 EP.

"We thought the footage was amusing and as usual if we think something is funny we wanna share it with everyone else. We don't want people to regard this as a tribute to Cliff because that would look as if we're trying to cash in on his death, which is far from the case.

"The film quality varies from the top-notch stuff done by TV companies to bootleg videos we tracked down which were often recorded by one kid standing out in the audience. This latter type of presentation gives a totally different perspective to the hi-tech material most bands have on their videos. There are points where the fan shooting the show gets bumped and the camera loses its position, ending up showing part of our lighting rig, which is great. There are also some clips that were done by the band as well.

"It's a rather unique way of doing a long-form video, because most acts just film one show with five or six cameras and that's it. The only footage specifically done for this release was an interview that me, James and Kirk did about Cliff. But even here it's far more than us just sitting there saying things like, 'Oh, he was the greatest bassist in the world'. We simply sat in an office with one camera on us and drank and talked for a couple of hours; it has the definite Metallica atmosphere. We go on about how Cliff was always late and stuff like that. There's also film of Cliff shot by friends of his, which people will find interesting. **"**

LARS ULRICH, NOVEMBER 1987

"We're astounded by it (the success of *Cliff 'Em All*). As I've said many times before it was never meant to be as big as it's gotten – it's just something that we thought a few of our hardcore fans might find interesting. From our point of view it was like the *Garage Days* EP on video – you know, half-serious, half-joke. So when I hear all these sales figures – like 100,000 in America alone – it just boggles my mind. It just surprised the hell out of me. "

LARS ULRICH, SEPTEMBER 1988

"We came real close to doing a promo video for '(Welcome Home) Sanitarium' and 'For Whom The Bell Tolls', but at the end of the day we just sort of asked ourselves 'Why? What's the point?' But if we ever do get around to doing one, it'll have to be completely different from your typical bullshit video that you can see on MTV's 'Headbangers' Ball', because we don't want to be associated with all the other shit that's on there. **"** **LARS ULRICH, SEPTEMBER 1988**

"We really wanted to do a video in that fashion – unique, different, and us. It's so us. We really did feel we did it on our own terms. "

LARS ULRICH, TALKING ABOUT THE PROMO VIDEO FOR THE SINGLE 'ONE', MARCH 1989

VIDEOS

❝It's a nice, jolly little affair, isn't it?**❞**

LARS ULRICH, REFERRING TO THE SAME VIDEO, MARCH 1989

❝We've been avoiding doing a video for years. We have come close once or twice in the past, the nearest being for the song 'For Whom The Bell Tolls', which we backed out of making at the last minute. But somehow 'One' always seemed to lend itself to a visual interpretation, and we also felt it was about time Metallica took on the challenge of making a video...

❝We wanted our own appearance to be as low-key and subdued as possible. Yet we also felt that the shots of us live should be moody and reflect the intensity of the film. Thus we chose Bill (Pope, director) because of his previous work with the likes of Peter Gabriel, U2 and Sting. He spent a lot of time getting the lighting correct, giving it a certain eeriness through the use of a blue tinge. Bill also used some interesting camera angles, shooting all of us in ways that concentrated on various limbs, thereby emphasising the fact that the kid in the song has no limbs...

“We tried to strike the right balance between telling the story and allowing the song to be more than just background music. I think we achieved that...

“It's weird, I've been in a band now for some eight years and this was the first time I've ever mimed to one of my own songs! But overall, I enjoyed the experience. And it's fucking strange to have Jason Robards in a Metallica video!” LARS ULRICH, MARCH 1989

“One of the main things that the 'One' video did for us was show us how video isn't actually the evil Satan we might have thought it to be. As of now, there isn't a follow-up planned, but I do know that something will happen in the future. Between the sick minds of James, the management and us I'm sure we'll be able to come up with something again.” **LARS ULRICH, DECEMBER 1989**

“Our managers felt that he's (Wayne Isham) the best guy at doing videos, bearing in mind we like to guard our stuff ten times more than anyone else once we've come up with the concept. But yeah, if you sit down and think that he's the guy that's done the Bon Jovi videos then it obviously has a frightening ring to it!”

JAMES HETFIELD, AUGUST 1991

“We're a lot more comfortable about doing things that on the surface seem much more than the norm than ever before, but at the same time the fact that we are who we are means that we leave our own distinct feel, regardless. The first three or four videos we did were these huge concepts, weird abstract stuff, and all of a sudden videos five and six are these not-too-different-from-what-other-bands-do studio videos. But our personalities stamp 'METALLICA' over them and make them different.”

LARS ULRICH, AUGUST 1992

VIDEOS

Selling Out (Or Not!)

"What are we supposed to do? Just cater for a specific 200 people or so for the rest of our lives? We are playing in a band that is growing and keeps getting new ideas, and to us as long as we're powerful and have that energy and feel for our music, then it doesn't really matter what tempo we play at. People have their own opinions about our music and so do we. The only difference is we're the ones playing that music so I guess we have an advantage there!**"** **LARS ULRICH, MAY 1986**

"OK, there's always the odd letter or comment like, 'If you don't play ten 'Metal Militia's on every album then it's not Metallica and it's not good'. But we're doing what we're doing the way we feel at a certain time. The band had matured and we're still learning. If people think we're wimping out then fuck 'em, we don't need that kinda shit." LARS ULRICH, DECEMBER 1984

"I sometimes get uncomfortable when we're analysed too much, because I'm not sure that this is a band that should be analysed in that fashion. We're really still the same roaring drunks, which is why when people mention selling out it's bullshit.
"Unfortunately, that isn't always to do with the music, it's to do with other things and I know that from being a kid myself. It's like some people don't want you to get any bigger. If some kid in Bumfuck, Egypt, was the first kid on his block to be cool and discover a band and they get big, then he doesn't look cool any more and he tells the band they're selling out. If someone came up to me and said that they really, really, truly hated everything on the *Master Of Puppets* album, then that'd be cool because he'd at least be talking about the music.

“I have to say though that anyone who says we've sold out with our music is missing things. I mean, come on, give me a break! Can you say that 'Battery', 'Damage Inc.' and 'Master Of Puppets' are hugely different to *Kill 'Em All* and *Ride The Lightning* shit?” **LARS ULRICH, AUGUST 1987**

“It (criticism) can happen to anybody who does well. Peter Mensch (band co-manager) has been saying that for years. But as far as we're concerned it's like, go ahead, help yourself. If people want to start fucking with Metallica then let them try and tear the record apart - I still like it.” LARS ULRICH, AUGUST 1988

“Kids come up and say, 'How come you don't do *Kill 'Em All*? And I go, 'Yeah, I like that album too. But there's more to our music than that'. We still do it live, and when we play it we mean it, man. But we have those songs in the set already.” **JAMES HETFIELD, NOVEMBER 1991**

SELLING OUT (OR NOT!)

"We sat down and made a record (*Metallica*) totally from our heart and soul. Okay? No ulterior motives. Then we had a band meeting and said, 'If we shove that record down people's throats more than we ever have before, there's probably a lot of new people who'll be attracted to it'. So you sit there and go, 'Well, we haven't compromised anything about what we've done from an integrity point of view, in terms of creative aspect'. So if releasing three or four more singles than we have in the past will turn however many people onto what we're doing, and subsequently turn them onto what we've done before, then we're getting to more people. And apart from the guy in Nirvana who'll lie to you and say that, 'Uh, we don't want anybody to buy our records', 99.9 percent of people in bands would like people to hear their music and get into their band. That is a fucking fact.

"Where does the sell-out begin? The day you form a band! You're selling out by writing for a rock magazine! So we said, 'If we do every interview, every TV show, if we release these singles, if we have the record company pushing and pushing, if we go out and play 300 gigs, then maybe people will go for it...', and they went for it! But it wasn't because we said, 'Let's make some songs that will turn more people onto us'. It was, 'Wait a minute, we've just made a record that might not piss as many people off!'"

LARS ULRICH, JUNE 1993

"The record company said to us they wanted to release 'One' (as a single), but it's nearly eight minutes long, has 23 guitar solos in, so could we trim it a bit? I sat down with the track and thought about it, until I discovered a way of keeping what I thought the vibe of the song was, from subtle to overdrive. My whole view was that if taking the last guitar solo out could get the song to more people who would then buy the album, hear a fuller version and get turned onto Metallica music, then fine.

"We've proven that before this whole radio/TV overdrive thing started kicking in, we'd managed to do 1.7 million sales purely on the touring and vibe. We've shown once again that I think we can do this whole thing without depending on the radio/video medium, which to us is very, very important. If radio wants to step along for the ride, then by all means come along. But understand that these are our songs the way you see them. Now, if you can get airplay from them in that fashion then by all means please do, but don't expect us to present four songs on a silver platter for radio because that's not gonna happen. It'll be on our terms as always." **LARS ULRICH, MARCH 1989**

"I think a lot of people in America right now, because we have become confident with what we are doing, are saying that we are doing the same arena rock clichés that these other bands were doing. If people come and see us and think it's arena rock crap then that's fine. It doesn't affect me because I know what we are doing is something distinctly different from what everyone else is doing." LARS ULRICH, APRIL 1992

"There was a very famous meeting we had in Toronto, when we were playing with Aerosmith, Warrant and The Black Crowes, in July 1990. Me, James and (co-manager) Cliff Burnstein sat down and Cliff said, 'If we really want to go for it, we can take this to a lot more people. But that will mean we have to do certain things that on the surface seem like the same games other people play'. But we were the ones playing that game, which make us, Metallica, just doing something else. And it was nothing to do with the music, it was the way we handled everything outside the music. The idea was to cram Metallica down everybody's fucking throat all over the fucking world!" **LARS ULRICH, AUGUST 1992**

SELLING OUT (OR NOT!)

Thrash Metal

❝I think the first album fits into that category, every number going at 500mph. But you can't call songs like 'The Call Of Ktuku' Thrash Metal. 'Fight Fire With Fire' and 'Trapped Under Ice' are pretty much the ultimate in Thrash, I think. But from a musician's point of view I don't really like that term. It implies lack of arrangement, lack of song writing, lack of any form of intelligence. Thrash Metal to me is just 'open E' riffing for five minutes as fast as you can go. We do play very fast, but I think there's a lot more to our songs than just thrashing. We try and arrange and structure them with good breaks, tempo changes and choruses with melody lines.❞

LARS ULRICH, DECEMBER 1984

❝I've noticed there's been loads of so-called Thrash Metal bands coming through recently. Most of them just use 'speed for speed's sake' techniques, thinking that fast guitar work is the only criteria for producing energetic performances. We're chuffed to have had such an influence on these acts, but what you hear from most of them is riff upon riff upon riff. They ignore the virtue of writing good material, and at the end of the day it's the standard of tune you're capable of delivering that matters.

❝To us, it's more important to record numbers that people can hum when they wake up in the morning. Sure, we enjoy playing fast, but there's more to us than speed. Listen to the tracks on the new album. Only 'Fight Fire' and 'Trapped Under Ice' are what I'd term 'high speed numbers'. They both feature very fast snare drum work, and that's the only way to judge the tempo of any track. The rest of the LP is played at a medium pace.❞ LARS ULRICH, JUNE 1984

“Yeah, it (the Thrash label) irritates me a lot. If you take the two extremes on the new album (*Master Of Puppets*) – which in my mind would be 'Damage Incorporated' and 'Orion' – I think if you look at what's in between those extremes the amount of ground we cover is so big, so vast, it really pisses me off that anybody would want to stick us with one label.

“Yes, we do a few Thrash songs because that's the sort of stuff we really like, but that's not all we like to do, that's by no means the only thing we're capable of doing and doing fucking really well! In other words, we're not afraid to play a little slower sometimes, we're not afraid to throw in a melody or harmony, we're not afraid to prove to people that we are a lot more musically competent than what they might expect from a band with our special kind of appeal.” **LARS ULRICH, DECEMBER 1985**

“I don't think that the word 'Thrash' ever applied to us, anyway. Sure we were the originators of the style because of the speed, energy and obnoxiousness in our songs, but we always looked beyond such limitations and were better defined as an American outfit with European attitudes to Metal. I hate the notion of pigeon-holing in rock and if we have to be seen as anything then let it be a power-based Metal band. I mean, what is Avant-Garde, Death, Hate Metal anyway?

“Quite honestly, I'm rather fed up with the mentalities shown by so many Thrash acts; all they wanna do is play faster and faster. What does that prove? Anyone can concentrate on speed for its own sake, but this doesn't allow any room for subtlety, dexterity or growth. Metallica is always seeking to improve, which is why we are getting attention now.” LARS ULRICH, MAY 1986

THRASH METAL ”

❝These days there seems to be all these people that suddenly jump on something just because it's trendy, like going out and buying upside down crosses, spikes and whatever, and listening to new bands because they're new. I just think there's something wrong with this whole underground thing; not necessarily the bands but these so-called true Metallists. I mean it's like, 'Fuck this, fuck that, these people are posers', and it's just getting ridiculous. Who's to say who's posing or who's fastest? The borders seem to be so thin that it just seems impossible to pin any of it down anywhere and nobody really knows where those borders run. With the underground you're either Thrash or you're posing and there seems to be no middle ground. It's all a bit worrying.❞ **LARS ULRICH, MAY 1986**

❝**There comes a point when where you just can't keep up with Deathhammer, Slayerkiller, Witchhorse or whatever, because, well, you just lose track, y'know? Obviously I'll put on the Slayer and Megadeth albums when the mood suits, but I still think that stuff like old Discharge really pisses over any underground stuff I've heard over the last three or four years.**❞ LARS ULRICH, MAY 1989

❝I think we've been labelled Thrash Metal enough times to be not remembered as a ballad band.❞ **LARS ULRICH, AUGUST 1991**

❝**We don't listen to Thrash or Speed Metal 24 hours a day.**❞

KIRK HAMMETT, NOVEMBER 1991

❝That whole Thrash thing has never bothered me. The only thing that bothered me was that people would read it and then they'd lump us in with other bands. I mean, people can call us whatever the fuck they like, but at the end of the day there's the bands name and people should call us that. When people hear the word 'Metallica' they now know what our music's about.❞

JAMES HETFIELD, NOVEMBER 1992

Touring

❝It's not a rock'n'roll party 24 hours a day!❞ JAMES HETFIELD, JUNE 1993

❝Every minute of a touring day is taken up, either with interviews or meeting people from record companies or contest winners from radio stations. It's much more than just the stage show.

❝It would be too easy to lock up and shelter away, only give people an hour-and-a-half up there on stage. But because of the attitude we have of reaching out as much as we can and not turning anything much down, the whole thing takes up every awake moment of a touring day.❞ LARS ULRICH, MARCH 1989

❝We couldn't have a better support slot than this one (the Ozzy Osbourne tour of the US in 1986). Ozzy attracts a really extreme crowd and as we are the most extreme of the up-and-coming Heavy Metal bands. We are therefore getting the opportunity to play to exactly the right audience. The band is getting a 55-minute set each night and are being given a great reception. Metallica is getting first-rate treatment from the Osbourne camp. I guess big acts like him are beginning to realise that having a hot opening outfit, presented in a situation where they can play their best and warm up the audience, will inevitably make the atmosphere even more electric for the headliners.❞ LARS ULRICH, MAY 1986

❝The 'Master Of Puppets' tour was cool, with that graveyard set that looked like we were playing in the album sleeve. And hopefully we'll come up with a similar concept with the next album. We'll have a big light show because we all really like that idea, but fuck, it isn't gonna stop us playing the kinda places we wanna play. I think it's important for us not to become an arena band. The smaller venues are great fun for us and if we can't fit 8,000 lights into a

small place or something, then we'll just fit in what we can and do the gig.

"Metallica will never sacrifice stage bullshit for the venues we wanna play, and we just aren't the type of band that you sell as a live show. Without mentioning names, we don't need 50-feet tall dragons to sell our tickets, because live all we are about is vibe and energy and the people, and we won't ever detract from that." LARS ULRICH, AUGUST 1987

"On this tour we're not just doing the 60-date arena circuit, we're also doing the secondary towns, and then a bunch of places no fucker's ever heard of. The theory behind that is that we didn't wanna rely on radio or video to keep us going, so in true European style we decided to play every town that has an arena and wants us. By the time the tour is over in the US we'll have done nearly 200 shows, so you're effectively letting people know all over what you do.**"** LARS ULRICH, MARCH 1989

"I have to be honest about this and say that I think the whole 'mega tour' thing has been blown gloriously out of proportion. Iron Maiden... are a prime example of taking a tour and going overboard about what a pain in the ass it is to play for a long time. Now it might be for them the way they work, but I think it's too easy to allow it to be blown up. We're in our tenth month and to be honest I feel fine. I'm definitely not at the burn-out stage and, although I won't say it'll never happen, after ten months I'm fine. It's a fine line, but I kinda like the fact that you adopt something of a daily routine.

"When I say 'fine line', I'm saying you have to be careful not to allow it to become an auto-pilot thing; that'd be too dangerous. You obviously have to have breathers here and there. A few days

TOURING

off here and there to keep it from getting too monotonous and to allow you to clear your head. But I haven't found anything objectionable about these mega-tour things as long as you take the right precautions..."

LARS ULRICH, MARCH 1989

"Being on the road for 18 months on a tour like this (the 'Damaged Justice' tour) has very little to do with normality! But every eight weeks or so we take a short break and I think that gives everyone a chance to wind down a little. Also, we all watch over each other, and I think that's one of the key things, because if something gets really silly and things are going in a direction we don't like, then I think that we're all so aware of it that we'll instantly kick each other in the ass, and it stops.

"Even though when we're on tour it is hard to keep in touch with the real world or whatever, we don't lock ourselves in our hotel rooms for 24 hours a day, we still go out when we can and do the same shit as we've always done."

LARS ULRICH, MAY 1989

"What's cool is that by the end of the tour we'll have played all 50 states (of America), which is something a lotta bands don't do. They just do the 60-date arena tour, whereas we're taking in everywhere we can play right now. We were sitting in the plane and at the table that you eat off there's a map of the States. We worked out that we had shows booked in 48 states, but that we'd missed two that pretty much everyone forgets about: Burlington, Vermont, and Wilmington, Delaware. We wanted to book some shows up there, and we were told there were no arenas really to play. So we said, 'Fuck it, let's do anywhere just to play'. We've booked a club date in Wilmington and 2,000-seat venue in Vermont. It's actually quite exciting to have a club date when you've just played 118 arena dates in a row...**"**

LARS ULRICH, DECEMBER 1989

"I look at that ('... And Justice For All') tour as a kind of awakening, seeing what we could and couldn't do, especially me. I found that I couldn't fucking drink like I used to, as far as singing went and being 100 percent into what the fuck you're doing every night and stuff. And just going that far, there's a point where you feel, 'Aw fuck, we've got a gig tonight', and kinda just go up and go 'La-la-la', and then you think to yourself, 'Well that's no fucking good', because you see other bands do that and you can always tell what's going on. So you learn when you have to quit for a bit, go home and take a break.

"I dunno, you sometimes wonder to yourself, 'Just what the fuck am I doing this shit for?' When it's been going a long time you think, 'Fuck, we could just go home right now'. But there's always something the next day that spurs you on and keeps you going.**"**

JAMES HETFIELD, MAY 1990

"We're bored! We're bored with staying home. And every time we see each other it's all we can talk about – you know, what happened on tour and how much fun we had... I mean, it's fun being at home, but it's also fun being out on the road. And every time we go to a big local show, like Aerosmith or something, we just want to get up there on stage so bad it leaves us feeling restless and impatient to get back together again and start playing." KIRK HAMMETT, MAY 1990

TOURING

❝It was pretty difficult, getting the 50/50 thing together, agreeing on a stage, times, where we're playing – there was a lot of shit that had to back and forth. It reminded me of buying a car; you're sitting there bartering with the guy, you start one side, he starts over on the other, and you meet in the middle.❞

JAMES HETFIELD, TALKING ABOUT THE METALLICA/GUNS N'ROSES
TOUR OF THE US, AUGUST 1992

❝I've always wanted to play with these guys (Guns n' Roses), ever since we met them in 1987. I've always wanted to – maybe more than the other three guys. I'm the one who's had all the late night conversations with various members of Guns.

❝Back in '87 we were the bigger band, then they became the biggest band in the universe. Now, in the hard rock scene of 1992, we're the two biggest bands. Taking the two biggest bands from one genre of music and putting them together on a tour is unprecedented.

❝The four of us are incredibly egotistical, end of story! Guns n' Roses are incredibly set in their ways too, and that's just the way it is. I don't think any of us realised, when we sat down and had our drunken talks about doing this tour together, how tough it'd be to get the three months of this happening. It's down to the persistence of the band members that this is happening, because if it was left to the managers, agents and accountants this would never have got off the ground. Whenever we had a stumbling block, we'd all sit down and work it out. We probably got to a point where we were being too petty about every detail – like the shirts and the passes and whatever all had separate Metallica and Guns versions, with each on the left on the top, or whatever. If that's the kind of stuff it takes to get the tour off the ground, then peace!❞

LARS ULRICH, TALKING ABOUT THE INFAMOUS GN'R TOUR, AUGUST 1992

❝We've got it pretty well worked out at this point. My body's fine, my brain maybe not and my throat's always the first to say, 'Fuck you, it's time to go home and take a break!' Being out for eight weeks at a time is enough. It's easy to get trapped on the road, so you just do it as it best works for you.❞ JAMES HETFIELD, AUGUST 1992

"It is sad; you're gonna miss some of these people, but it's no different to being at school or in a job for two years. There's no doubt that we've experienced a lot on this tour."

JAMES HETFIELD, TALKING ABOUT THE END OF THE
'WHEREVER I MAY ROAM' TOUR, JULY 1993

"I don't think we were showing the crew the appreciation we should've. They were working real hard, and when you get to the point that you only notice the stuff that's going wrong – 'This water's not hot enough' or 'This stupid little thing's not right' – and you blow up at them, it ain't cool. But when you're in a rut and everything's the same every day, the only stuff that stands out is the bad shit, and you don't realise how much great shit they're doing the whole time. We kinda got lost in ourselves, but then everyone did – you get mesmerised by the road and get into this rut that you have to break out of.**" JAMES HETFIELD, JULY 1993**

"We were on our way to Adelaide (on the '... Justice ...' tour)... we had this chartered plane and one of the engines cut. We were almost there actually, but instead of just going on we turned around to go all the way back because that's where his tools were to fix the fucking thing! We basically started freaking out..."

JAMES HETFIELD, NOVEMBER 1991

"When you're touring by yourself with no one pushing you, it can be hard to inspire yourself. Whenever I say that to Jason he tells me I'm a fucking dick, though we all feel like that every so often.**"**

LARS ULRICH, AUGUST 1992

TOURING

❝I look in the itinerary and there's two more pages of crew than there was last year, there's more people wandering around the hallways with laminates on that you don't know the names of...❞
LARS ULRICH, JUNE 1993

❝... I was pretty much afraid of travelling, flying and touring for a long time. I was afraid to go too far from home – I thought I'd lose my base or whatever. I lost my fear of flying on this tour (the 'Wherever I May Roam' tour). I mean, we pretty much flew everywhere, and the scary thing is that I kinda got to enjoy travelling towards the end of the tour!**❞** **JAMES HETFIELD, JULY 1993**

❝I could go on and on – I'm not looking forward to going home. This is what I'm here to do; I'm here to play guitar, to play shows... that's my vocation in life, and just going home and doing nothing makes me feel guilty, like I'm a bum or something.❞
KIRK HAMMETT, JULY 1993

❝310 gigs... Am I tired? Yes. Burnt out? Yes. But am I having a good enough time to deal with it? Yes. It's been an incredible ride, and I feel good about what we've done. I'm burnt as hell, but when we go up there for three hours we play better and better every day, and that side of it is good. The 21 hours off stage is not as easy to deal with...**❞** **LARS ULRICH, OCTOBER 1993**

"We've been through so much. We've been to totally obscure places few rock bands have been to, like Manila and Singapore... and that in itself was an event. We ventured into unknown territory and in many cases were the first rock band there. We didn't know what was going to happen and they didn't know either. It was a virgin situation and that made it very interesting. It's different than playing 200 ice hockey arenas in North America.

"There were always 500 or 1,000 people at the hotels, so we were prisoners. We couldn't go for a walk around the corner. We needed a police escort and travelled in groups of 20 people, much bigger groups than we're comfortable with, but it was necessary. We spent four days in Jakarta and I saw the hotel, the venue, and the Hard Rock Cafe..." LARS ULRICH, OCTOBER 1993

"I can't think of anything right now that makes me feel this tour is over. It seems like we're going home on a break, and we'll go back out in a couple of weeks playing more shows somewhere!"

LARS ULRICH, JULY 1993

"It is strange because it does just feel like a break in the tour. After the last show I had a couple of bottles of wine to myself and ended up throwing up before my flight..." JAMES HETFIELD, JULY 1993

"There was a point when we were just adding on more tour legs and I just said, 'Forget it, I'm not going any further, I'm *sick of touring!* I don't have to justify myself or argue the point, I'm just humanly sick of it!'" JAMES HETFIELD, JULY 1993

"It's been an incredible ride for the last three years. Everything's exceeding our wildest, drink-induced expectations. I'm happy about everything from the sales point of view, the gigs we've done, that people give a shit, and that I'm still here to talk about it! It's been so cool. So much positive stuff has come out of it, and so little negative. There were times on the tour I thought it would never end, and now I can see the light at the end of the tunnel."

LARS ULRICH, OCTOBER 1993

TOURING

"I'm absolutely flabbergasted (on learning of the Metallica/Limp Bizkit/Linkin Park/Deftones Summer 2003 US Tour). Do they really think it'll sell them more than a couple of fucking thousand tickets if Linkin Park – or whoever – are on that bill? No, there are people out there who still want metal, and it's too bad it wasn't addressed in that way." **JASON NEWSTED, APRIL 2003**

"They (Metallica) had the opportunity to come back as leaders, to take out (on the road) bands such as In Flames, Strapping Young Lad and Voivod – bands that deserve to be seen. Metallica are the only one with that kind of opportunity." JASON NEWSTED, APRIL 2003

"Everyone is fucking psyched and pumped up. The guys in Linkin Park told me it was an honour to play with Metallica because they grew up listening to us. To hear something like that from a musician you respect, who is carving their own way in music, is a pretty cool thing; it lifted me up and gave me a lot of enthusiasm." **LARS ULRICH, FEBRUARY 2003**

"Ultimately, I want to be able to go out and see Fred Durst do his thing and watch John Otto play drums, and then go back to the dressing room and put my little silly shorts on and go up onstage and take that energy with me. Knocking on the door of 40 as I am, the competitive stuff has worn thin and I'm just happy to be part of the musical landscape rather than trying to take it over."
LARS ULRICH, JUNE 2003

"We played a festival in upstate Michigan in probably the most torrential rainstorms I've ever seen. It was just pissing from the moment we went on. But you know what, it was a total vibe for us, if not the audience." **JAMES HETFIELD, JULY 1999**

Success

"I think the general attitude of this band is to make the most of a current situation and never to look forward too much. To be totally honest I've never looked forward and said, 'Oh yes we'll have limos and be selling-out huge venues'. We live much more in the present on a day-to-day basis.

"It's no secret that the financial situation has changed, and the way in which you travel from point A to point B affects the way the music comes out on stage. I think we do try to make sure, since this tour started, to be as comfortable as possible without being stupid about it...

"Yes you do get spoiled with things like your own plane. Some stretches of the tour we've had our own plane, which means we can make our own schedules, and I'm not whinging now at all, but going back to commercial travel from that situation is something that lets you know you're spoiled." **LARS ULRICH, MARCH 1989**

"I kind of freaked myself out at how huge the band has got over here in the States... I've been out in the middle of nowhere, fishing on the road in Winnipeg or somewhere, and some fucking guy will come up and say, 'Can I have your autograph?' And then it's over! There's just all these different people, and it does end up getting annoying. I can be nice to people of course – I can sit and talk to people about something else – but it's always questions like, 'How did you write this song? How did you do this?'" JAMES HETFIELD, AUGUST 1992

"I guess we know this band is starting to get genuine success because not only have we got two bottles of vodka per night on our dressing room 'rider', but this isn't the cheap stuff we've been used to – rather, it's Absolut!" **LARS ULRICH, MAY 1986**

"I haven't had a shower for three days, man. I've only just thought about it. I think it's got something to do with success; the more successful you are, the less you feel like washing."

LARS ULRICH, AUGUST 1987

"I don't think our success has changed us as people at all. We are still the same lunatics as when this band first got going and never see ourselves as being on a higher level than the fans, but there are so many of them now displaying an interest in Metallica that we are being stretched.

"For example, after a gig all of us enjoy meeting the kids and signing autographs, but it becomes a real exercise when there are about 4,000 of them surrounding the tour bus. The demand on your time increases enormously.

"We have also begun to check into hotels under pseudonyms because everyone knows where the band is staying as our bus is parked right outside, and if the fans have access to you all the time then you'll be constantly disturbed at any hour by people trying to get passes for the following evening's show and so forth. Surely, even a successful rock band must have a certain amount of privacy?**"** LARS ULRICH, MAY 1986

"I know it's standard corny answer number five to say that 'success hasn't changed us', but it hasn't and it can't. A lot of

that is down to each of us keeping the other in check, and also down to our management team. They don't allow things like that to affect us, they keep our feet on the ground if they have to, which isn't really that often...
"I think a lot of that 'star' bit is very much down to oneself. We're just the same drunken idiots next door we've always been, we don't throw barriers between us and the kids."

LARS ULRICH, AUGUST 1987

SUCCESS

❝There are so many gold, platinum and silver discs arriving at my house that I'm thinking of moving to a larger place!**❞**

LARS ULRICH, MARCH 1988

❝Anyone who says they don't want to see their record in the chart is full of shit!❞ LARS ULRICH, AUGUST 1988

❝At last we're a Top 40 band!**❞** **LARS ULRICH, MARCH 1989**

❝I think the only way Metallica is an arena band is statistically. Our mentality and the way we look at things most certainly isn't that way at all. We'd be just as happy to play clubs and whatever.❞ LARS ULRICH, DECEMBER 1989

❝One of the first things people say to me now is, 'Hey, you guys are real rich?' Who gives a shit?**❞** **JAMES HETFIELD, NOVEMBER 1991**

"You think one day some fucker's gonna tell you, 'You have a Number One record in America' and the whole world will ejaculate. I stood there in my hotel room and there was this fax that said, 'You're Number One'. And it was like, 'Well, OK'. It was just another fucking fax from the office.
"It's really difficult to get excited about it. We've never been really career-conscious. We never tried to be Number One. But now we're Number One it's, like, OK."

LARS ULRICH, NOVEMBER 1991

"I never pictured in my mind what having a Number One record meant, because I never thought it was possible to have a Number One record with the kind of music we play.**"** JASON NEWSTED, NOVEMBER 1991

"We're not an overnight success. It's not like all of a sudden you've got all this money and it alters your attitude and ego instantaneously. We've been able to kind of grow with it and evolve with it and really learn how to handle things."

JAMES HETFIELD, FEBRUARY 1992

"When you're an overnight success, it sucks. It throws all your responsibilities and your perspective completely out of proportion. Things tend to blur. Hitting fast is way harder to handle than the steady climb. I mean, when you hit too fast, all of a sudden every little insecurity you've ever had, you instantly want to blow them out of the water, because this new success, you see, means you have to start acting accordingly, which is bullshit.**"**

KIRK HAMMETT, FEBRUARY 1992

SUCCESS

METALLICA *Talking*

"I guess it's an honour. Next to Hendrix and The Doors, huh? That's pretty scary!"

JASON NEWSTED, COMMENTING ON METALLICA'S INDUCTION INTO
CIRCUS MAGAZINE'S HALL OF FAME, APRIL 1992

"Every time this happens to a band, you know, that success comes so quickly, as it's now happened to Nirvana, or when it happened to Guns n'Roses, I really am thankful that things happened one step at a time for Metallica. Every album was bigger and bigger. I know what Guns n'Roses went through and it was really difficult for them to deal with it. And even now, you know. There are a lot of things happening with Metallica right now, but for us it's not that difficult to deal with because it's just a continuation of what's been going on for the first eight, nine years. Within the band everything is pretty much the same, the only difference is that outside of the unit there's a lot more craziness." **LARS ULRICH, JUNE 1992**

"On the road you get so pampered. Everybody around you works for you and that's a dangerous environment."

LARS ULRICH, SEPTEMBER 1991

"(Success is) ...being able to play what we want and not having to conform to anybody and still coming through and over, and still being accepted. Being true to ourselves, that's what it comes down to." **JASON NEWSTED, NOVEMBER 1993**

"In America we seemed to have reached a different level. We have been one of the biggest metal bands on the scene for a while, but now we're up there with those bands whose appeal is very broad and transcends pigeon-holing. There's ourselves, Guns n' Roses, MC Hammer, U2, Michael Bolton, Garth Brooks... We all sell to a wide cross-section of people." LARS ULRICH, FEBRUARY 1992

"It's like we're living in the middle of the eye of a hurricane, wondering what the fuck is happening. We seemed to have remained inside of what's going on. It's like a spectacle to us. We're watching all this activity around the band, and it just doesn't seem to

touch us. We still wake up with hangovers and are late with interviews. The only tangible change has been the number of girls turning up at our gigs, which in America is a sure sign that you've crossed over. And the amount of people trying to get backstage.

" I don't think we have changed as people, despite all this attention. I'm perhaps not the right one to ask about egos, but I don't honestly believe any of the four of us have changed because of the success we are enjoying. Oh sure we have altered as people, but that's more to do with the passage of time and growing as people. We are not the same now as we were as 21 year-olds, but then you can say that about anybody. **"**

LARS ULRICH, FEBRUARY 1992

" You try to evaluate it (success) as best you can... it's a fucking lot more difficult. Everybody's trying to get at you, and there's a lot more shit to do, a lot more people to please. I've never really liked people very much anyway. Overall, it's harder to keep in contact with the folks who are coming to your show, and hear what they have to say about it. "

JAMES HETFIELD, AUGUST 1992

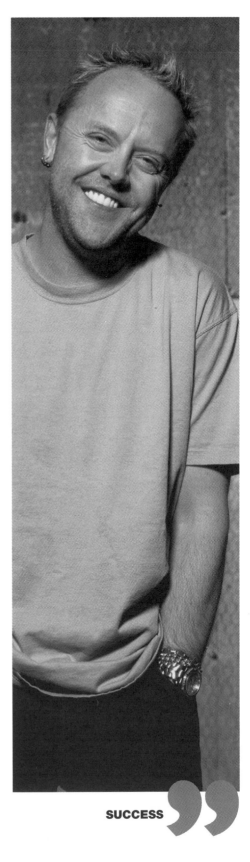

SUCCESS **"**

66 The more I think about it, the more I realise that we've probably survived the most difficult time that any band has to go through; that transition from when you're not kids any more. And, all of a sudden you're a lot bigger than you realise. If you can get through that – look at any of the bands out there, from Guns to Mötley Crüe to Maiden to Anthrax to Poison, all going through line-up changes and shit. We really have a solid thing going on within the four of us, and we've survived the changes of the last three or four years. We're through that tunnel of potential trouble.

66 Yeah sure, I've always had this (thick-skinned) personality, but before it was, 'He's really eccentric and dedicated and stubborn in a positive way'. Now that we happen to be one of the biggest bands in the world, all of a sudden it's, 'He's got a huge ego'.

66 Okay, yes, we're big. Yes we make a shit-load of money – more than we should. Corporate? No, because we still deal with 95 percent of what goes on ourselves. We still get off on what we do – anyone can challenge me on that, anyone that knows us can see what's going on, in our faces and in our emotions when we're playing. The minute that we don't, I doubt that we'll continue.

66 Of course it's different from ten years ago. Metallica is big business, and the minute you try to deny that you're fucked. We directly employ 75 people on the road, and we are responsible for dozens and dozens of people in offices and stuff around the world. But, we also had those companies back in '84, the difference is now we're making enough money to fucking pay 'em! A lot of those people worked for free back then because they believed in what we were doing. 99

LARS ULRICH, JUNE 1993

"The champagne, the caviar! No, I don't like to exploit it (the band's success). If a photographer comes out to do photos of us, I'd rather not see photos of us in our plane. I mean, who gives a fuck? That's not how we wanna be perceived. Sure, we've got a plane and I don't mind talking about it; we get from point A to point B quicker and get more rest in between, that's all."

JAMES HETFIELD, AUGUST 1992

"By the time our four-year cycle is over, this album (*Metallica*) will probably have sold about ten million copies worldwide; it's rearing its head towards nine right now. So where will we go from there? I have no fucking idea where we'll go from there!

"I don't know if we'll have another record this big, but I know that we'll walk out of the studio after the next Metallica album with the same hard-on that we had for Metallica albums one to five. And, as long as I'm happy about it, what difference does it make?

"I've got all the money I need. I could retire tomorrow if I wanted to. It's not about money any more. It's about egos; I wanna go out there and be the biggest band in the world and sell more records than anyone else. And I'm not gonna compromise that for anything." **LARS ULRICH, AUGUST 1992**

SUCCESS 99

Starting
Over

"We'd been off the road since last summer and, after resting for a few months, started getting bored and restless. We started jamming and did an MTV competition winners thing where we played and hung with two fans for a couple of days; that got us going again, and Lars really wanted to go out and play. We made a few enquiries and, the next thing you know, there's a whole summer tour booked..."

JASON NEWSTED ON THE SHIT IN THE SHEDS TOUR, JULY 1994

"The phone started ringing right about when we were about to record, and we couldn't focus on it. Every two weeks there'd be another phone call, so I called up James and said this could really be a lotta fun. It took James and I about 30 minutes to talk ourselves into it.

"This isn't about three months of rehearsal or having to have the perfect set list. It's about having fun, and it's in keeping with the looseness we've achieved in the new songs. We thought that spirit would carry over really well to Donington. It's going to be a case of 'Hi... we're in the middle of making a record and here we are in front of 80,000 people!'"

LARS ULRICH ON HEADLINING THE 1995 DONINGTON FESTIVAL, AUGUST 1995

Metal v Britpop

"With this whole Seattle thing, it's like the attitude has been driven out of hard rock in the last four or five years. I like Soundgarden, I liked Nirvana, some of Pearl Jam's stuff, but where's the attitude? Oasis are the first band in five years to have excited me to the point where I consider myself a total punter again. Oasis are a really great hard rock band with attitude, but Blur do nothing for me...**" LARS ULRICH, AUGUST 1995**

BRETT ANDERSON OF SUEDE

"Suede kicks ass! Their first album is so rock it hurts... They came over to my house and stayed till five in the morning, drinking and doing whatever. And we jammed. We played a bunch of David Bowie songs, Iggy Pop songs and T-Rex songs. Brett Anderson was an ordinary bloke and he didn't spank his buttocks once!"

KIRK HAMMETT, OCTOBER 1996

"How would I feel about being a gay icon? Who asked that – the singer from Suede?"

JAMES HETFIELD, DECEMBER 1996

"I don't think I've ever been less interested in music outside Metallica than I am right now. Nothing inspires me, I'm totally into what we're doing, but all I listen to is Slade at the moment..." LARS ULRICH, AUGUST 1997

"I like Radiohead's *OK Computer*. Kirk had been raving about it and I thought I should check it out. It's got some cool moments musically. They create some great moods on the record; I can't get that fucking 'Paranoid Android' riff out of my head!**"**

JAMES HETFIELD, JANUARY 1998

"If I put on Napalm Death or anything super-heavy, Lars will just walk out of the room. It's not something he's into any more. He'll still bang about the place to the first Iron Maiden album, or the Tygers Of Pan Tang. But when it come to new stuff he's not really that hip... he's more interested in other things."

JASON NEWSTED, DECEMBER 1998

STARTING OVER

"Jason thought he was happening, and how he's the resident hippy! Hair's become so fucking useless to us. This is the shortest my hair's been since I was born."

JAMES HETFIELD ON JASON HAVING THE LONGEST HAIR IN THE BAND, MARCH 1996

"I think we all feel a lot more comfortable about not being so trapped in what bands like us are supposed to look like."

LARS ULRICH ON THEIR SHORTER HAIRSTYLES, MARCH 1996

"Make-up ain't my thing, but Kirk loves it. He can wear a goddamn diaper on-stage, I don't give a shit. It's his choice. He's a fucking grown man, and who am I to say don't fucking do that. Well I'll say it, but it don't mean shit. He can make himself look an ass and I really don't care."

JAMES HETFIELD, OCTOBER 1996

"The whole image thing was such a laugh, the haircuts and all that. It was just too hot for long hair, and with a little bit of hair loss here and there they decided it was time to trim it. The guys are in their thirties now, and we all know what happens to hair when you get older...**" TOUR MANAGER 'BRUMMIE', NOVEMBER 1997**

"I wish I could have done it ten years ago. I mean, this is the best thing I've done, ever, in terms of comfort, plus I've started smoking. I wish I'd started smoking ten years ago and I wish I'd cut my fucking hair ten years ago, it could have been a whole different story! I think smoking kind of mellows me out..."

LARS ULRICH, NOVEMBER 1996

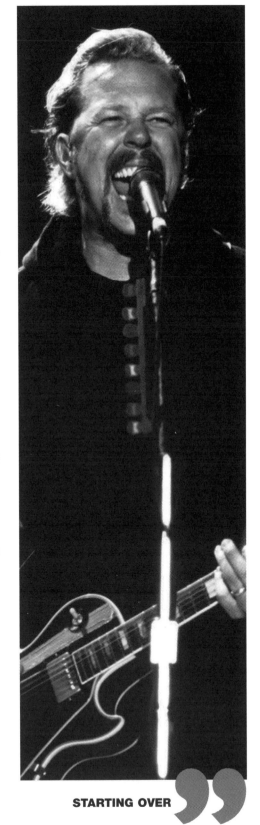

"Realising that I don't need booze all the time is kind of a cool thing. It wasn't a big deal and still ain't. There are friends of mine going 'What's the matter with you, you pussy?' but I just tell 'em I'm sick of drinking. I got tired of planning my day round hangovers. I don't miss the hangovers but I miss the taste of beer, so I drink Coors Cutter non-alcoholic."

JAMES HETFIELD, DECEMBER 1997

"I really have no respect for people who have no respect for other people's right to be different, or even be different from how they were five years ago. That kind of intolerance annoys me, and makes me want to push it a little bit more in their face to piss them off."

LARS ULRICH, NOVEMBER 1996

"Metallica haven't changed much – I mean, Hetfield still wears black..."

MANAGER PETER MENSCH, 1997

STARTING OVER "

Older...&
Wiser?

❝Guys relate to their moms, I think, a bit better than their fathers. When you're singing about Mom, it's like... what are you gonna say when you're getting into a fight with some guy. You say: 'Hey! Your fucking mom blew me!' That hits home, it's a little deeper, gets you a little more upset. Hur, hur.❞

JAMES HETFIELD, NOVEMBER 1996

LARS WITH HIS WIFE, SKYLAR

❝I have a great relationship that I've been in for almost a year now, and I've purposefully tried to change a lot of the things about my personality that I didn't like in order to try and not make the same mistakes again.❞ LARS ULRICH, JANUARY 1997

❝When I proposed, we'd known each other for 254 days, so I had it set up that they would bring out 255 roses – one for each day we had known each other, and one for the future.❞

LARS ULRICH, DECEMBER 1997

❝I really feel that the rock star thing is out of my system. I lived it, loved it and embraced it for many years, and had a great time with it, but not any more. I prefer to hang out with my wife.❞ LARS ULRICH, NOVEMBER 1997

❝I was trying to sneak the (engagement) ring out onto the table without her looking. But that never really worked out, so I told her she had some spinach in her teeth and to go into the bathroom to sort it out. Hur, hur! Then when she came back I had the ring set up with a note and all that fancy bit... she thought it was a joke, of course!**❞** JAMES HETFIELD, DECEMBER 1997

❝I think there's agreement that the tour doesn't have to be two years long – an overall acceptance to other parts of life. Metallica is the number one love for us, and all the women in our lives know that. So there's a lot more time gonna be spent creating our own family, which has been missing.❞ JAMES HETFIELD, NOVEMBER 1997

❝(Producer) Bob Rock has, like, 35 kids and they're always hanging out in the studio. James is great with them. He also has a niece who he's really good with. So I haven't noticed any major changes with him since fatherhood, he's always been great with kids.
❝I'm welcoming the challenge of parenthood. I know it will change me, because everyone says it does. I think it'll continue to calm me down...**❞** LARS ULRICH, AUGUST 1998

❝Seeing the birth of my daughter was no grosser than gutting a deer, so I could handle it. You go through every fucking emotion there is... wonder, then crying. The baby comes out and starts crying, so you lose it. Then you're all puffed up cos you're a Dad. That was probably the biggest experience of my life.❞

JAMES HETFIELD, DECEMBER 1998

❝Most places the fans are always trying to get to you, and now we're so close it's like, 'Oh, I can touch him.' But after seeing all the pyro (fireworks), they don't fucking dare go on stage. But that's what we missed, getting close up. I want to play at fucking eye level.❞

JAMES HETFIELD ON TOURING, OCTOBER 1996

❝It's a lot more intense than the last show we had. If you're not in the right place at the right time you could get killed, and that kinda adds an edge to it.❞ KIRK HAMMET, OCTOBER 1996

❝It's still the band that plays all the fast, ugly shit live. It doesn't matter if they're wearing shirts that cost 200 bucks where they used to cost 20, it's still the same dudes. Even if we're not creating that super-fast shit on tape, we're still capable of it.❞

JAMES NEWSTED, OCTOBER 1996

❝I didn't want to be in a situation where we always have to top what we did last time, and obviously the show we played for a year and a half on the *Load* album was pretty big. So you'll find these gigs are pretty minimal in production. It's just us playing for two and a half hours. There's some video screens, some pyro, but no major effects up there.❞ LARS ULRICH ON TOURING, AUGUST 1998

The New Millennium... & Beyond

❝This show has a lot of sentimental value to me. I'm very proud to be playing the biggest place in my home state on the biggest day of the century. It's an honour to be on the same stage with Ted Nugent, who was one of my heroes growing up as a musician in the 1970s.❞

JASON NEWSTED ON THE NEW YEARS EVE SHOW AT THE PONTIAC SILVERDOME, MARCH 1999

❝**For those who believe that the year 2000 is the beginning of an era, not the end of the world, what better way to celebrate than with Metallica, the Defiant One, and his buffalo? Y2K this!**❞

TED NUGENT, ON THE SAME SHOW.

❝I think we're going to skip a year. James and I were just talking about it last night, that we'll be able to sit down for the first time in six years and have a situation where we don't have any

THE MILLENNIUM... & **BEYOND**

dates in front of us. It's a luxury, but we've worked our asses off, and it's time to just chill out. I think everybody could use a break from Metallica for a year. Get the fuck out of the way for a while. **99**

      LARS ULRICH, OCTOBER 1999

66 I've got a lot of stuff on tape because I haven't submitted anything since October '96 or whenever we put the songs together for *Load*. I've had some deciphering to do, and I've learned so much about what works for James's singing and so on. 99

      JASON NEWSTED, DECEMBER 1998

66 There's a difference between having aspirations and chasing them. I'm not the next guy in line to chase movie parts, or pushing the script I've been working on for five years – but if somebody came to me and said, 'You'd be perfect for this', under the right circumstances I'd be game. I'm at a point in my life where I would welcome almost anything creatively. **99** **LARS ULRICH, OCTOBER 1999**

66 I've been thinking a lot about the next record the last couple of months. I'm starting to get very excited about proving we can and will reinvent it once again and come up with something unlike anything you've heard from us. There are a lot of new things that have come up that we can draw inspiration from. Whatever happens, I know the next Metallica album will sound like a total natural Metallica album for the year 2001. But it will be once again, very different. I look forward to getting on with that some time next year. 99 LARS ULRICH, OCTOBER 1999

Farewell Jason

"During the last couple of tours he (Jason Newsted) was totally withdrawing from everything. Going into his own little world, wearing headphones all the time, never communicating, and we certainly weren't kings of communication either. We were just four guys who would shut up, play and let the beast roll on."

JAMES HETFIELD, 2003

"I think that if Jason had just stuck it out for two or three more days rather than coming to that one meeting and saying 'I'm out of here, no questions asked', things would have been a lot different to the band." LARS ULRICH, AUGUST 2003

"You don't know what home is until you leave, and he'd (Jason Newsted) maybe have become more grateful to be in Metallica. That's certainly one ending to that story. But that certainly wasn't the only reason that he left. A lot of other things combined and caused him to escape into a future of his own elsewhere, and search for happiness. And we're all hoping that he finds it."

JAMES HETFIELD, AUGUST 2003

"We were ambassadors for American music in many, many places. We took that kind of music to places that had never seen it before." JASON NEWSTED, MAY 2003

"I don't feel Jason was happy in Metallica, and maybe he's forgotten some of that. Maybe a lot of the glamorous parts are missing from his life now and reality is kind of really sinking in now. We want to help him through that."

JAMES HETFIELD, MARCH 2003

FAREWELL JASON

"Jason was overlooked. And the ironic thing is that the model for what would have been the perfect Metallica in Jason's mind is the one that exists now. That is kind of ironic. It's also a little sad, because Jason's a good guy and he put a lot of effort into the band for many years, and in retrospect he was never really fully accepted into the band. Then when he tried to go elsewhere to satisfy his creative needs, he was told – well, barked at – that he couldn't. He was caught in no man's land. So in a way he sacrificed himself – or had to be sacrificed – in order for us to be able to move to the place we're at now. So it's ironic, and really sad. For me, it's amazing that it lasted for 14 years, that Jason stuck it out for that long." LARS ULRICH, AUGUST 2003

"To this day I'm still pissed off at Jason for leaving."
KIRK HAMMET, 2003

"The hard work that I've been a part of, making this great thing Metallica for a long time, is something I'm very proud of. I've been out for more than two years now, and I look back on some of the videos and on some of the photographs, and it looked pretty cool, man, and it looked pretty metal. I like that. You're supposed to look back and say, 'Fuckin' right on!'" JASON NEWSTED, MAY 2003

"There were some times that sure freaked me out, in the way that we were treated like king and queens. We'd sit down for dinner with prime ministers." **JASON NEWSTED, MAY 2003**

"The music was hard to learn and I was under a lot of pressure in following Cliff – but there was way more good stuff than bad."
JASON NEWSTED, APRIL 2003

"Metallica have a really dry, sarcastic humour and they do say 10 per cent of sarcasm is truth." **JASON NEWSTED, APRIL 2003**

"The vertebrae in my neck and spine are cracked, after 15 years of windmilling. I was definitely an innovator – if there is such a thing as the art of headbanging – but now I'm paying for it."
JASON NEWSTED, APRIL 2003

"Metallica are the kings of metal and we need them to continue to set the standards. As a fan of Metallica, I only want to see them kicking ass again." **JASON NEWSTED, APRIL 2003**

"I have full respect for Jason, I would never try to take the place of Jason Newsted in this band because he's a tremendous player and he was an amazing key figurehead in this band. This is a new Metallica now, and I'm happy to be a part of it."

ROBERT TRUJILLO, JUNE, 2003

"Through the years, whenever people have talked about them (Metallica) in the underground or in interviews, somebody always said that they were ahead of their time. I think it's absolutely true." **JASON NEWSTED, MAY 2003**

FAREWELL JASON

Metallica
Vs Napster

"I don't care if people don't like me personally, but this is an important issue. There are very few forms of media where we can sit down like this and explain exactly what's at stake here. Most of my comments on this have been reduced to 30 second soundbites which is why people are asking, 'Do they really need more money?'" **LARS ULRICH, JUNE 2000**

"The ideal situation is clear and simple – to put Napster out of business."

LARS ULRICH, JULY 2000

"Do we need more money? No we're fine. Thank you for asking about my financial situation, but I'm taken care of for 10 fucking lifetimes."

LARS ULRICH, JUNE 2000

"We felt that it was morally wrong and we had to take a stand. I find it strange that people who know Metallica and how we like to control what's come from us, think it's weird that we're going after this. We don't pick fights but we felt that a line had been crossed. And when somebody fucks with us we deal with it." LARS ULRICH, JUNE 2000

> "We take our craft – whether it be the music, the lyrics, or the photos and artwork – very seriously. It is therefore sickening to know that our art is being traded like a commodity rather than the art that it is."
>
> **LARS ULRICH, APRIL 2000**

> **"If the requirement of being a Metallica fan is that I give you music for free, I don't want you as a fan. Go away, leave us alone."**
>
> LARS ULRICH, JULY 2000

> "Why is it only people who've computers have the right to free music? Should all music not be free then? Can we just throw the doors open at Tower Records and do away with the cash registers? It doesn't make sense." **LARS ULRICH, JUNE 2000**

> **"Everybody talks about the Metallica backlash, but 'I Disappear' has been the most requested song on radio for five weeks and we've sold 400,000 tickets for our 12 US dates this summer, so I wonder if this backlash is from the same people who had fucking heart attacks when we cut our hair, or when we got Bob Rock to produce our *Black* album."** LARS ULRICH, JUNE 2000

> "Obviously Metallica aren't going to go out and start chasing after people, but at the same time, what's happening is illegal."
>
> **LARS ULRICH, JUNE 2000**

> **"Contrary to popular belief, we're not some sort of finger-wagging believers in the anti-piracy thing. It's just standing up for Metallica, which we have always done throughout every aspect of our career."** LARS ULRICH, JUNE 2003

METALLICA *Vs* **NAPSTER**

❝We're trying to educate people to the fact that what they're doing is wrong.❞ **LARS ULRICH, JUNE 2000**

❝**If people grab songs from the internet and then don't buy that record, it's going to be really tough for new artists to break through record company channels, because when the record companies see that the sales aren't going up they'll withdraw their support.**❞ LARS ULRICH, JUNE 2000

❝We were in a position, unlike almost every other contemporary artist, where we had an exclusive contract since 1990. We didn't need to use the record company as a bank and Metallica has funded everything it's done, every album, every video. That's why we were so vigilant. No one else has their own music to protect.❞

JASON NEWSTED, AUGUST 2002

❝**It's a pain in the ass. Doing interviews and research on this takes up four hours each day, which is time I could spend playing with my son. But I have to remind myself that the reasons I'm doing it is because it's the right thing to do.**❞ LARS ULRICH, JUNE 2000

❝You can accuse me of many things, but one thing you can't accuse me of is not always having the best intentions of Metallica at heart.❞ **LARS ULRICH, 2003**

Rehab

"We started to write, and then as we were going deeper into ourselves, and exploring why it was that Jason left – what it meant to us, and all of that – it started stirring up a lot of emotions and a lot of stuff about how we could better ourselves as individuals. So I made the decision to go into rehab." **JAMES HETFIELD, AUGUST 2003**

"Things weren't working for me. It affected family life, it affected band life, it affected everything that went on around us."

JAMES HETFIELD, AUGUST 2003

"It's more like a realisation – mid-life crisis, identity crisis, whatever you want to call it – that the world doesn't revolve round me as the dude in Metallica. That was my identity and my worth. My worth was confused with my mission in life. I've got a lot of new attitudes towards life." **JAMES HETFIELD, AUGUST 2003**

"You'd try to escape that feeling, but no matter where you went you were identified as that guy in Metallica. And, as corny as it sounds, you take that on. You kind of submit to it, and you're signing autographs when you're trying to eat dinner with your kids, or having photos taken when you're on vacation. But you don't have to do that. Any human would say 'Can you leave me alone for a second?'... There's some good things that I take from my past, but I've found a new love for my life as me, instead of as the guy in Metallica." JAMES HETFIELD, AUGUST 2003

"The expectations are immense. And I don't have to live up to those expectations. You're out on the street, walking around, and someone wants you to jump around and act like a clown like you do on stage... I'm not that way all the time. But when you don't meet their dreams of the person they believe you to

REHAB

be when they finally meet you, it's difficult for them;
it's difficult for people to understand that the dude's a
human, you know, because they've built you up into some
king, god-like thing. And it's tough to live up to that. **"**

JAMES HETFIELD, AUGUST 2003

**" We hadn't heard from James… and I had to think of a back-up
plan. I'm the kind of person who always needs back-up plans or,
as my therapist says, exits, escape routes. So I sat down and
thought about it long and hard, and thought 'do I have enough
things in my life to fill the void if Metallica is gone?' And it would
have been a drop, right back down to the ground. It would
virtually have been like starting over for me. And after realising
that I could, it gave me enough confidence to wait things out
rather than just panic about the situation. "**

KIRK HAMMETT, AUGUST 2003

" James is a changed man. But it's good. His eyes are clear.
He's always been the most honest person I've ever known, and
that's still there and it's still pretty serious business, but we hadn't
sat together, just the two of us, without anything else
going on, in ten years.
So we finally got to sit
down for two hours, just
hang out for a second, and
talk. It was good. We're
brothers, man. There were
always two dressing rooms
for Metallica: Kirk and Lars,
and James and Jason. We
were together all the time,
and he's still the person I
respect in music more than
any other. **"**

JASON NEWSTED, FEBRUARY 2002

“After Jason left... the other guys certainly spun the wheels in their heads wondering how to control their futures when it wasn't up to them – it wasn't up to any of us, really. But coming to that realisation was important. It made us stronger as individuals, and it gave us real perspective on how much we mean to each other and how much we'd taken each other for granted.”

KIRK HAMMETT, AUGUST 2003

“There's a thread from James Hetfield treating Jason like that, and realising his mistakes and going into rehab. Not necessarily an obvious, direct correlation, but there is definitely a link in there somewhere. In some sub-conscious way, something happened.”

LARS ULRICH, AUGUST 2003

“It's like James had a problem processing a lot of the thoughts and feelings he had, and Jason leaving was one of the feelings he had trouble processing. It's been a huge learning experience, and something that Jason set in motion for all of us. He was the sacrificial lamb for our spiritual and mental growth as well as our creative growth, and it just sucks. It's medieval.”

KIRK HAMMETT, 2003

REHAB

Road To Recovery...

"Just leaving rehab was scary. Going through some absolutely cathartic experiences in seven weeks there, and elsewhere up to a total of three months, and then coming out into the world was scary... I didn't want to forget about all the other stuff that had to happen... how we're not going to be going on two-year tours any more; my family is important to me, I can't let my children grow up without me; and all the other priorities, how they lined up in my life... We all started taking a look at ourselves and becoming a lot more respectful of each other and our needs."

JAMES HETFIELD, AUGUST 2003

"I didn't go in rehab but I had help in figuring out what I needed to do. I was having some problems which stemmed from childhood that were affecting how I was conducting my adult life, and going into therapy and getting to the bottom of that explained why I did drugs in the first place. There was a pattern of abuse when I was a child that made an indelible impression on my psyche."

KIRK HAMMETT, JUNE 2003

"James has pushed himself to another level as a human being – the metal's back in Metallica." **LARS ULRICH, FEBRUARY 2003**

"My wife had a surprise party for me, and I saw this guy standing in the corner, casting a familiar shadow. And it was James. I was so fucking glad to see him, and I could instantly see from looking into his eyes that there was a new clarity there, a new awareness and a new sensitivity that I didn't detect before. It was totally amazing. We were able to exchange a few words, and I was able to make sure for myself that he was okay and functioning on a somewhat sane level. But he told me 'You know, it's still going to be some time.'" KIRK HAMMETT, AUGUST 2003

"There was a period that we had to go through to adjust to the new James Hetfield. And it was just as much of an adjustment for him as us." **KIRK HAMMETT, AUGUST 2003**

"There was a whole dynamic change that had to happen within the group. And certain things had to shift... One person changes and everyone else around them, all relationships, friends - everything changed." JAMES HETFIELD, AUGUST 2003

"I had to reintroduce myself to those guys and they didn't know what to think... To them, to my wife, to everybody."
JAMES HETFIELD, AUGUST 2003

"Lars, (producer) Bob Rock and I had to continue getting together for meetings just to keep the faith, keep the momentum going and just keep in touch. Because everything was falling apart around us, but we felt that if we held strong and held it together, at least we had each other." KIRK HAMMETT, AUGUST 2003

"There were times when I seriously thought Metallica was over."
JAMES HETFIELD, AUGUST 2003

ROAD TO RECOVERY...

"James had his vision of the perfect family, and it's almost kind of mafia-style; you're part of the family, and if you step outside of the family you're betraying the family, and you'll get ostracised. And that is at the heart of a lot of the stuff that we've tried to work through in the last couple of years."

LARS ULRICH, AUGUST 2003

"In the last two years we've been exploring our inner personalities and discovering that there's a lot of fucking residual anger there that came from our childhoods, and it's something that fame, money and celebrity is not an antidote for. It's deep-seated anger that's always been there."

KIRK HAMMETT, AUGUST 2003

"I've been trying to dump everything else – sex, drugs, rock 'n' roll... chocolate's a real struggle these days – or work."

JAMES HETFIELD, AUGUST 2003

"You know, in rehab I saw it all; people taking certain behaviours to extremes, to where it becomes an addiction; compulsive activity that just started to ruin their lives. Anything can really be taken to that extreme. But I'm comfortable with the unknown right now, and trusting of it, so life is filling that hole. Life on life's terms is okay for me." **JAMES HETFIELD, AUGUST 2003**

"I've gone through life trying to avoid struggles, either drink them away or hide from them, but being able to face them and take them on knowing that you are going to grow after you've walked through the fire and be okay, all of these things that we have been talking about have made us stronger as people and as a band." JAMES HETFIELD, AUGUST 2003

"The downside to alcohol for me is too huge.**"** JAMES HETFIELD, JUNE 2003

"I've recently said that rehab was college for my head, but really I meant to say that it was college for my soul."
JAMES HETFIELD, JUNE 2003

"I wouldn't say that my goal in life is to be happy all the time, because that's an impossible goal, but I'm more comfortable with being down...**"**
JAMES HETFIELD, JUNE 2003

"The months and months of the guys going round in circles waiting for me when I didn't even know whether I was gonna be back must've been very hard."
JAMES HETFIELD, JUNE 2003

"I have a drink occasionally, but the nose keeps itself a lot cleaner these days than it has in the past. I can still fire it up when need be – particularly when Rob (Trujillo) is around.**"** LARS ULRICH, JUNE 2003

ROAD TO RECOVERY...

Metallica Now...

66 I can see how someone could get caught up in that fear of running out of creative juice. 99 **JAMES HETFIELD, AUGUST 2003**

66 On *Kill 'Em All* there's no doubt we had it – we were friends and brothers in arms out there battling against 80's big hair bands – it feels really good to be strong again. 99 JAMES HETFIELD, JUNE 2003

66 The mood in the band reminds me of when I first joined 20 years ago. When I first joined the band there was a huge infusion of new energy. Up until Cliff (Burton) died we were just so psyched about everything and life in general. But that kind of ended when Cliff left. 99 **KIRK HAMMETT, AUGUST 2003**

66 **I have to say the future looks so great I have to put sunglasses on.** 99

KIRK HAMMETT, AUGUST 2003

66 Here's to the future of Metallica. We're an icon, but we sure ain't done yet! 99

JAMES HETFIELD, MAY 2003

66 **My mind-set is to go out there and show the world how strong Metallica is.** 99

JAMES HETFIELD, FEBRUARY 2003

"We went through the meat grinder, but we're still together and not just a fucking quivering piece of hamburger in the corner. It's always darkest before the dawn." **KIRK HAMMETT, AUGUST 2003**

"Music was a great gift for me, and I discovered that somewhat early. But I don't need alcohol, I don't need anger, I don't need serenity, I don't need any of those things to be creative."

JAMES HETFIELD, AUGUST 2003

"This is the healthiest Metallica has ever been. I thing we've another strong ten years in us. And to be where we're at right now, with all of us able to look into each other's eyes and say; 'I love you, bro', that's a special thing." **KIRK HAMMETT, AUGUST 2003**

"We don't need to go around hugging each other to prove to ourselves what good friends we are." JAMES HETFIELD, MARCH 2003

"One of the biggest misconceptions about Metallica is this whole thing of 'We're doing it for the fans.' No, we're not fucking doing it for the fucking fans, we're doing it for ourselves!"

LARS ULRICH, JUNE 2000

"Yes, we sign autographs and we're accessible and we don't put ourselves on pedestals above our fans." LARS ULRICH, JUNE 2000

"I don't want to turn into a cabaret act, which is why we continue to fuck with ourselves, fuck with our audience and fuck with our songs as much as possible. It's not turning into a joke. When it does, I'll be the first one out of here." **LARS ULRICH, MAY 2000**

"I'm just so glad to be doing this again." LARS ULRICH, MARCH 2003

"It's never done unless you're done. And we haven't said we're done yet." **JAMES HETFIELD, MAY 2003**

METALLICA NOW...

"We've still got it. We've still got it." LARS ULRICH, MARCH 2003

"We're Metallica. What we do is not something you can turn on and off like a switch.**"** **JAMES NEWFIELD, MARCH 2003**

"No matter how much you mature there's still a boy in you that wants to have their clubhouse."

JAMES HETFIELD, MARCH 2003

"I feel bad about the way we were in the past.**"**

KIRK HAMMETT, MARCH 2003

"In San Francisco, every second person you see is pierced, and I just didn't feel like being one of the legions of pierced people. These days I feel more of an individual without them."

KIRK HAMMETT, 2003

"The problem with Metallica in the '90s was that we never slowed down long enough to take stock of what was going on, and all the personal relationships became secondary to the Metallica machine.**"** **LARS ULRICH, JUNE 2003**

"Having my family on the road is going to be more positive, where it used to be pretty negative because I'd push them away. Now I can see what great things they bring me." JAMES HETFIELD, JUNE 2003

"It's interesting how familiar my wife Francesca and Lars are in personality, I can see why I've been drawn to those people.**"**

JAMES HETFIELD, JUNE 2003

"It's pretty interesting to hear my lyrics sung by a female (on Avril Lavigne singing 'Fuel' at live MTV)." JAMES HETFIELD, MAY 2003

"Metallica isn't ready to turn into some nostalgic shit.**"**

LARS ULRICH, MAY 2003

Rob: New Kid On The Block

❝I hate clichés, I really do, but there's no way around this, it really does feel like a new beginning for Metallica. The energy that Rob brings to the party is incredible. He has an almost zen like quality to him that Metallica really needs. And no disrespect to previous bass players, but Rob's work sits in a very different place, it feel's more like a proper unit.❞ **LARS ULRICH, JUNE 2003**

❝**I was overwhelmed (on being asked to join Metallica). I was buzzing, of course, it was an absolute high point.**❞

ROBERT TRUJILLO, MARCH 2003

❝My mother listened to a lot of Motown, which was great for a bass player because that's the prominent instrument. My father was listening to the Stones. But my cousins listened to Sabbath, and I remember listening to that and thinking they were possessed.❞

ROBERT TRUJILLO, JUNE 2003

❝**When I walked into the room the guys were clapping, everyone who worked in the office was clapping, and I was just like 'Wow'. And they said 'Have a seat. We know in our hearts that you're the guy for the job and we want you to become a family member of Metallica'.**❞ ROBERT TRUJILLO, MARCH 2003

❝You have to understand that my relationship with Ozzy and Sharon (Osbourne) has been very strong for seven years. And as much as I was buzzing about the Metallica thing, I was also aware that I was leaving a situation with my other family that has been so good for me. They're great people and I love them, but this move comes with their blessing.❞ **ROBERT TRUJILLO, MARCH 2003**

"After I'd absorbed the Metallica thing the very thing I did was to gather my thoughts and call Sharon (Osbourne) and explain what had happened and how I felt. Both Sharon and Ozzy were totally cool about it. In fact Ozzy called me a couple of days later to congratulate me he was like 'Good on yer, fella, they're a fookin' amazing band!" ROBERT TRUJILLO, JUNE 2003

"Robert is the best choice (Metallica) could have possibly made. He is solid and musical, he knows his shit and his style is very strong. He's also a strong-willed person — strong physically and mentally. He's got a big heart and a good family. All of those things are important to be able to put up with something as huge as the Metallica entity, and he's got what it takes. I'm excited to see Metallica live now, man. As a fan, I wasn't sure Metallica could be able to come out and be a force again, but now that they have Robert I think they will. If Robert and James can click the way I think they can, they could be a huge, huge thing."

JASON NEWSTED, MAY 2003

"(On Not Playing On 'St. Anger') People say to me, 'Why didn't they have you re-track the bass on the record?' But Bob Rock's bass playing on this stuff is amazing. He's a part of the way these songs have been written, and it wouldn't be right for me to step in there. I'm just happy that the guys let me play the songs for the DVD part of the album, they've been really solid on making me feel part of this new album as much as possible."

ROBERT TRUJILLO, JUNE 2003

"With the greatest respect to Jason, there's a difference between replacing a member who has left and replacing a member who has died." **LARS ULRICH, MARCH 2003**

BOB: NEW KID ON THE BLOCK